THE PUCK STARTS HERE

The origin of Canada's great winter game

ICE HOCKEY

GARTH VAUGHAN

**Goose Lane Editions and
Four East Publications**

Published by Goose Lane Editions and Four East Publications with the assistance of the Canada Council, the Department of Canadian Heritage, the Nova Scotia Department of Education and Culture, and the New Brunswick Department of Municipalities, Culture and Housing, 1996.

Back cover: Photograph of Garth Vaughan © Sherman Hines, reproduced with permission. Starr Skate poster courtesy of Dalhousie University Archives.
Edited by Lisa Hammett Vaughan and Charles Stuart.
Book design by Paul McCormack.
Printed and bound in Canada by Gagné Printing.
10 9 8 7 6 5 4 3

Canadian Cataloguing in Publication Data

Vaughan, Garth
        The puck starts here

        Includes bibliographical references.
        ISBN 0-86492-212-4

1. Hockey — Canada — History.   I. Title.

GV848.4.C3V38 1996   796.962'0971'09   C95-950254-8

Goose Lane Editions
469 King Street
Fredericton, New Brunswick
Canada E3B 1E5

Contents

Dedication

Ice hockey originated in Nova Scotia, where it developed over three-quarters of a century before spreading systematically from east to west and becoming Canada's national game. This book is dedicated to the pioneers of the game:

The boys of King's College School, who adapted the field game of hurley to the ice of Long Pond in Windsor, Nova Scotia, c. 1800.

Nova Scotia's native Mi'kmaq craftsmen, who carved, from hornbeam trees, the hockey sticks with which the game was played as it evolved in the early and mid-1800s.

John Forbes and Thomas Bateman, who invented the Acme Club Spring Skate at the Starr Manufacturing Company in Dartmouth, N.S., in 1865, which revolutionized skating and ice hockey.

James George Aylwin Creighton of Halifax, N.S., who introduced ice hockey, hockey sticks, and the Halifax Hockey Club Rules to Montreal in 1875 and who also contributed in large measure to the development of ice hockey in Ottawa in 1884.

Cadet #149, Roddy McColl of New Glasgow, N.S., and others, who taught hockey skills to fellow cadets at Royal Military College, prior to the first RMC-Queen's game of 1886 in Kingston, Ontario.

Acknowledgements

A retired surgeon would not be my first choice to write a book on hockey, especially if he hadn't held a stick for 50 years. So, when I decided to write this book, I realized that, if I was to score, I would need as many assists as possible.

My daughter, Lisa Hammett Vaughan, encouraged and assisted me, and edited the material. In the distant past, I helped with her early education. Recently, I have gained strength, and learned much from her, and I have loved every minute of our shared experience.

To my daughter, Kate Hammett Vaughan, who took time from her vacation to help with editing and typing, thanks for the effort and the fun that we had.

To Howard Dill, sports historian and my friend since childhood, I am grateful for his enthusiasm about my project. For our discussions concerning all manner of things regarding the history of ice hockey and the pioneers of the game, for the loan of books, magazines, and photos from his lifetime collection, I offer sincere thanks. He's a joy!

In 1988, on the occasion of the bicentennial of King's College School (King's-Edgehill School), Gordon Hughes of Windsor arranged a press announcement regarding the origin of ice hockey that attracted attention to the school and town. Our discussions, and his encouragement regarding the research for the writing of this book, are appreciated.

My sincere thanks to Phil Etter and Ken Pemberton, close friends who separately spent hours of discussion with me early in my research project, and helped strengthen my conviction to do the job I felt needed to be done for Nova Scotia — that of recording the story of the evolution of ice hockey in our province. I am also grateful to cousin Phil, a writer and editor, for continued guidance in the writing of the material.

Leslie Loomer, historian, researcher, and writer, has always been helpful with information, opinion, and welcome advice. It was Leslie who researched the John Cunard information.

Dale Rissesco helped with research. I enjoy his continued interest and our discussions.

To Marie (Sexton) Purnell Musser, my friend from Mifflenburg, Pennsylvania, who allowed me to use her article describing her early experience as a hockey player in Nova Scotia, I am indebted.

To Ron Caplan, whose article on making stock skates takes us back a couple of generations and reveals a different way of life, I am grateful for the privilege of including his writing in this book.

Archivists at Dalhousie, Harvard, King's, and Queen's Universities, and the Royal Military College, the Public Archives of Nova Scotia, Prince Edward Island, New Brunswick, Manitoba, Quebec, and the National Archives of Canada, as well as the Curators of the Dartmouth Heritage Museum, Randall House Museum of Wolfville, and the West Hants Historical Museum at Windsor, have been consulted, and all have been most cooperative. I am grateful for permission to publish photographs and other material from the collections of the Nova Scotia Sport Heritage Centre (NSSHC), the Provincial Archives of Alberta (PAA), the Public Archives of Manitoba (PAM), the Public Archives of Nova Scotia (PANS), Queen's University Archives (QUA), Royal Military College (RMC), West Hants Historical Society Museum (WHHSM), and the Windsor Hockey Heritage Centre (WHHC).

I am pleased that the late C. Bruce Fergusson, Nova Scotia provincial archivist of Port Morien, Cape Breton, researched our hockey heritage and focused attention on it in an article that was published in the *Nova Scotia Journal of Education* in 1965.

Patti Hutchison and Tommy Sweet at the Nova Scotia Sport Heritage Centre shared knowledge, printed information, and photos, and offered encouragement and advice, which I appreciate.

The keen memories of Windsor's long-time residents, my dear friends Katherine "Kay" Anslow, Bertha (Kuhn) McHeffey, Peter "Pete" MacKinnon, and H. Carleton "Cy" Smith, have been of immeasurable assistance — recalling names, events, and details of our proud hockey heritage. They are all honorary members of the Windsor Hockey Heritage Society.

To members of the Mi'kmaq nation, Rita and Noel Smith, Alexander "Sandy" Julien, and Raymond Cope, whose own stories and those of their ancestors have enriched the material for the book as well as my own life, I am sincerely grateful.

To Jim and Helen Wilcox, for lending material about their uncle, Blaine Sexton, who spread the word and technique of Canada's great game in England, my thanks.

Dr. Sandy Young, Head of the Department of Sports Education, Dalhousie University, has long been teaching students about Nova Scotia's proud ice hockey heritage. From him I gained inspiration to record the facts about our heritage which I find so fascinating.

To J.W. "Bill" Fitsell, of Kingston, Ontario, author of *Hockey's Captains, Colonels, & Kings*, noted journalist and researcher of hockey history, for his book, friendship, advice, and his gift of material and photos, I am very grateful.

Brian McFarlane, host of *Hockey Night in Canada* for 27 years and the author of many books on ice hockey, is an inspiration. Brian has been very helpful with discussion, direction, and encouragement. Our association has been interesting and fun-filled.

Al Hollingsworth, journalist, TV political commentator, and provincial hockey league executive, who shared memories of our town's proud hockey heritage, gets full marks from me!

David Swick kindly assisted with the book title.

I am grateful to Richard Rogers, of Four East Publications, whose interest in my project led him to seek me out, and to the staff of Goose Lane Editions, who brought the book to completion.

A very special thanks to my wife Lauren, who ushered me into the computer age by lending me her lap-top and teaching me how to use it, and who listened to every paragraph (and the replays), and checked each picture and caption, even though hockey is not her thing. Thanks for both your interest and forbearance. (You learned a lot!)

To my family and friends who have heard little other than *hockey* from me for the past four years, I hereby solemnly swear never to mention the "H" word in your presence again. Unless!

GARTH VAUGHAN

Prologue

Stricken with hockey fever during my youth in the 1930s, I made stand-up cutouts of my NHL hockey heroes Syl Apps, Gordie Drillon, Turk Broda and others, and admired them on my bureau. I had hockey cards under my pillow and in my school desk, and I talked hockey with my friends incessantly. CBC radio with Foster Hewitt and *Hockey Night in Canada* was a must on Saturday nights (even if I did sometimes fall asleep and have to get the final details from friends at Sunday school the next day). The rest of the week, the local town hockey and regional Valley League activity consumed as much of my time as homework and chores. Hockey activity in my home town at the time was almost more exciting than I could stand. I was hooked on hockey.

Little has been recorded regarding the formative years of the game, when it was played for recreation, for fun, and for amateur competition. In the 1930s, ice hockey was a very exciting part of life for many people. Nobody seemed to know, much less care, where the game had come from. Most were content with accepting that it had simply arrived on the scene. I had an insatiable desire to know what went on before my time. Fortunately, personal contact in the 1930s with our local hockey legends gave me insight into hockey for at least the two previous decades. Knowledge about ice hockey prior to that time seemed to be foggy.

My search for information concerning the origin of ice hockey proved to be long and difficult. However, the information I found about the evolution of the game, and the equipment with which it is played, is so interesting in its own special way that it made the effort rewarding to say the least.

Coffee table editions of books depicting the glamour of the game and its heroes, for the most part concerned with happenings surrounding the NHL and the Stanley Cup, appear annually and thrill

Syl Apps

me as much as they thrill my fellow fans of the game; however, words about the game in the very early years are scarce and hard to come by.

The story of ice hockey as we know it today consists of two parts: (1) the development of the game after it was first played in Montreal on March 3, 1875, about which much has been written, and (2) the origin and evolution of the game that occurred for at least 75 years before that very important date. My particular interest, since retiring from a 30-year career as a general surgeon, has been to return to my childhood interest in ice hockey and search out the facts concerning the early part of the story — things that I've always wondered about. Recording the results of that quest, along with describing amateur hockey in my home town in the early 1900s, is my purpose in writing this book.

Garth Vaughan
October 1996

Gord Drillon

Foreword

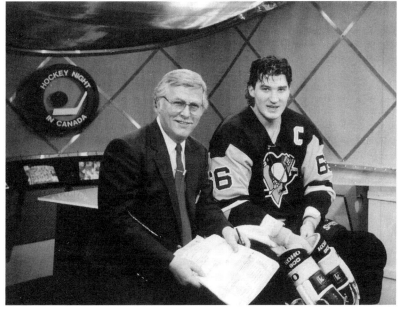

It was good news for hockey fans when my friend Garth Vaughan, a prominent Nova Scotia surgeon, put aside his practice in 1990. After decades of performing surgery and writing prescriptions, he decided to devote his retirement years to a subject dear to his heart, and to the hearts of most Canadians — hockey. He has spent years probing the game and its Maritime roots. And what a treasure-trove of fascinating facts he has uncovered and chronicled in his dedicated quest. Fans curious about the heritage of the game that millions now watch, play, and enjoy will find much satisfaction in the pages ahead: there's the evolution of hockey's rules and equipment, the dilemma faced by goalies standing between two stones (guardians who could be scored on from all directions by opposing hockeyists using hornbeam sticks and wooden pucks), the construction of covered rinks, the little-known story of the first Black hockey league in the world, and overdue recognition for the stickhandling legends of Maritime hockey.

Perhaps most important, the good doctor makes a convincing argument in support of Windsor, Nova Scotia's claim to be called "Hockey's Birthplace," with evidence dating back almost 200 years. At the same time he wields a nifty scalpel and systematically demolishes the lingering and somewhat ridiculous claim that the game first evolved on the harbour ice in Kingston, Ontario.

The Puck Starts Here is a welcome and worthy addition to the fast-growing library of books on hockey. It fills a rather large void, providing vital information about our hockey heritage and its Maritime pioneers. For fans like me, cursed with a thirst for more and still more hockey information, Dr. Vaughan has prescribed an immensely satisfying elixir. It's good medicine, Doc. Thanks and congratulations!

BRIAN MCFARLANE
HONORARY PRESIDENT
SOCIETY FOR INTERNATIONAL HOCKEY RESEARCH

Introduction

It is fitting that a retired doctor has ended the longest gestation period in the history of mankind and finally delivered from the womb of disputation the absolute proof on the birthplace of hockey.

The Puck Starts Here is an eye-opener. Not only does Dr. Garth Vaughan put to rest the debate on the "birthplace of hockey," he does so by weaving the interesting supportive data, historic background of Windsor, and local colour into a lively must-read for all fans of the game.

As a native son who spent my first 17 years in Windsor, I was surprised and, yes, embarrassed at what I was reading. Too many times I shook my head with an "I didn't know that." When you are young you don't usually have "lighthouse vision." Thankfully, Garth did, and still does, see everything around him.

I skated on all the ponds mentioned, and some that were not. It was a time, a much simpler way of life, such that wherever there was ice, a pick-up game broke out. For the record, Windsor has produced many outstanding hockey players. I was not one of them. We played, not because we had visions of the NHL in our eyes, but because we loved the game. We had to endure the pain of feet jammed into cramped second-hand skates and protected only by outdated catalogues or magazines taped to our shins for protection.

The ultimate was to skate and play at the Windsor Rink, a bandbox with natural ice. To those unfamiliar with the rink and the times, Garth's descriptions of the bizarre happenings may seem far-fetched and written with a heaping helping of imagination. Not so. These things, so many forgotten, are true. Thanks, Garth, for bringing them back and for finally proving to the world where this great game of hockey had its start.

AL HOLLINGSWORTH
JOURNALIST, SPORTS WRITER, AND
NOVA SCOTIA PROVINCIAL HOCKEY LEAGUE EXECUTIVE MEMBER

Boys have a pick up game of hockey
outside Windsor's old natural ice
rink, built in 1897.

Garth Vaughan

CHAPTER 1

Hurley to Hockey in Nova Scotia

Windsor

VIEW OF WINDSOR FROM HALIBURTON'S HOME — Thomas Chandler Haliburton's home, Clifton, overlooked Fort Edward, the busy Avon River with its shipbuilding yards, and the town centre, a world-renowned port of registry and seaport visited by ships from all over the world.

W.H. Bartlett

When Tom Haliburton was a boy attending King's College School in Windsor in the early 1800s, skating and playing "hurley-on-ice" on Long Pond were the favourite winter pastimes. Ordinarily hurley is a fast, competitive game played on a field with sticks and a ball. In Ireland, where hurley originated, the weather allows the game to be played year round. For three seasons of the year, fields in Nova Scotia are also suitable. However, when winter arrives and fields are snow-covered and rough, hurley becomes impossible. The boys at King's College School adapted the game to the smooth, steely hard ice of Long Pond, their regular skating spot, just in back of the college grounds. All they had to do was to clean the snow from the ice with their scrapers and shovels, as they did each day for skating anyway, grab their hurleys, and go to it.

It was lots of fun, and they played it as much as time would allow. They had to quit and leave Long Pond before dark to get back to the

HURLEY STICKS, PRE-1920S —
The early "hurley" stick and the
early "hockey" stick were almost
the same. They have both changed
over the years.

National Museum of Ireland

school in time for supper, for they did not have outdoor lights. The trail led back through the college woods past the Frog Pond and the Devil's Punch Bowl, two of their other skating places.

Hurley-on-ice certainly made life around King's a lot more interesting through the winter. Just imagine the excitement in Halifax when boys who were attending King's went back home to their city friends and taught them the new ice game that they were playing at school in Windsor!

Halifax and Dartmouth

The boys in Halifax and Dartmouth got as excited about playing hurley on the ice as the Windsor boys, and the game soon took over the ponds and harbour inlets in Halifax and the lakes in Dartmouth. There were lots of Irish settlers in the Halifax and Dartmouth area, as well as in Windsor, and they would have been excited to see the children adapting the Irish field game to ice. The young boys played it first, but it wasn't long before the older boys and men and members of the military got interested and involved. Skaters were unsympathetic and certainly didn't appreciate these hurley players cutting across in front of them and messing up their style. They especially disliked the younger boys who were trying to learn the game, and who darted in and out, tripping, falling, and sprawling all over the ice with their hurleys. The bigger guys didn't care to have the kids around while they were playing a serious game, either. The young boys who liked to show off their skill, seemingly coming from nowhere, would grab the puck with their hurleys and race away into the distance, bringing the game to a halt. And when one of the players gave chase and was closing in on the young thief, the boy would simply shoot the wooden puck off in one direction, and scurry off in another, out of harm's way. The kids were hard to manage, but their ability to control the fast-moving puck marked the beginning of the art of stickhandling. They were fast becoming "puck-hogs," and that was the aim of every young aspiring player, then and now. When the game became more popular and the boys were wanting to play it on Sundays, a lot of parents and most of the clergy got upset because it interfered with Sunday school and church attendance. Many thought that the game was dangerous and should be forbidden.

Getting Rough Already

The game got a little rougher as the boys developed more speed and skill on the ice. It seemed to take on a character of its own before long, different somewhat from the game as it was played on a field. Injuries occurred, some due to body contact and high-flying sticks (just as they did on ground), and some due to skates. One injury that was talked about around the school for a long time was the story about a Halifax boy, John Cunard (whose family later developed a steamship line), who had his front teeth knocked out playing hurley on Long Pond. Pete Delancey of Annapolis, the student who wielded the wound-inflicting hurley stick, was reminded of the injury each time he met Cunard. It was a most unfortunate injury for a young student. Poor John's toothless smile would attest to the growing roughness of hurley for some time.

THE DUTCH PLAYED GOLF ON ICE —
Early paintings showed the Dutch playing golf on ice, not hockey.

Aert van der Neer (1619-1663):
Kanal im Winter
Rijksmuseum, Amsterdam

Same Game, New Name

Folks continued to play hurley-on-ice outdoors in Nova Scotia each winter, sometime calling it "ricket" as well. Then they began calling it "hockey" on occasion, and hurley or ricket at other times. Whatever it was called, the game seemed to grow more popular each season.

A Game Worth Sharing

For 75 years, ice hockey was played outdoors, on ponds and lakes, according to basic rules that were known to all involved. Beginning in Windsor, the playground of Halifax, the game quickly came to be known and played in Halifax and in the neighbouring town of Dartmouth. Before long, there were newspaper accounts of its also being enjoyed in Pictou and New Glasgow, 90 miles to the east. In those neighbouring towns, hurley was played on the ice of Pictou Harbour and the East River.

EARLY HURLEY INJURY IN PICTOU — Samuel Cameron was born in Scotland in 1814 and served with the Royal Highland Emigrants in Quebec. Following demobilization, he received a Nova Scotia land grant and became a young immigrant farmer in Pictou County. There he received a blow on his knee while playing hurley on the ice of the East River intervale. The knee later broke out in a chronic running sore which caused him to cease farming and take up teaching school as a means of livelihood. In 1845 Samuel travelled to Boston in search of medical help for his injured knee.

The Long Cross-Country Trip

The game was confined pretty much to that central area of the province until it was discovered by a visiting reporter from Boston, who returned home and excitedly wrote about it in the Boston *Evening Gazette* in 1859. That route of communication was natural because of the early, strong bond that had been established between the ports of Windsor, Boston, and Halifax. The Prince of Wales visited Windsor, Halifax, and Saint John in 1860, and is reported to have played ice hockey back home in England in 1863. By 1865, when the new Starr self-fastening skates were invented in Dartmouth, the boys in Saint John, New Brunswick, were playing hurley on their new Starr Acme Club skates. Ten years later the game spread to Montreal where it was very well accepted, making its public appearance on March 3, 1875. From then on it developed and spread more quickly than before. It had taken nearly three-quarters of a century for the game to evolve in Nova Scotia before it caught on in another Canadian province. After it was played in Saint John and Montreal, it took only 15 years to spread to the West Coast. Records show that folks began playing ice hockey in Winnipeg and Victoria in 1890. The game had endeared itself to young and old alike, and nearly every town and village across the nation had become involved by the turn of the century.

Made in Nova Scotia

Nova Scotia was the first province in Canada to be developed and a lot of things happened there before they happened elsewhere in the country. It's little wonder that the country's pioneers developed the national game in Nova Scotia. Just as they developed the game, so Nova Scotians devised the basic rules and the equipment with which the game is played: wooden pucks, Mic-Mac hockey sticks, and Starr skates. In the final decade of the spread of hockey from east to west, the familiar wooden, shingle-covered rinks popped up everywhere. Canada's new game was invited to come in out of the weather, from the natural ice surfaces of its origin. Finally, in 1899, with the game established from coast to coast, the Nova Scotia box net was invented, as if to complete the set of equipment used in the game before the first century of play came to an end.

CHAPTER 2

Early Hockey in Nova Scotia

The Evolution of the Game

Ice hockey was not invented. Rather, it grew or evolved gradually from hurley-on-ice. Chances are, the boys in Windsor played their first game on Long Pond just as it is played on the field, wearing boots or shoes. If putting the game on ice was stage one of the process, then playing it on skates was the second step. When wearing boots, it's difficult to stop quickly or turn on ice, while the use of skates facilitates sudden and speedy changes of direction. Imagine the excitement of the boys of King's College School starting to play hurley on skates on Long Pond. It would be the natural thing to do because, after all, Long Pond was their favourite place to go when they wanted to skate.

"THREE CHEERS FOR LONG POND" — It was boys at King's College School who first played hurley, the forerunner of ice hockey, on Long Pond in Windsor. The pond was a favourite skating place then and remains so to this day. Having just finished a "pick-up" game of hockey, these young Windsor boys salute those who started the game which they love so much.

Garth Vaughan

CAPTAINS CHOSE PLAYERS AND END — **Children from all parts of town gathered together and played hockey on the many ponds.**

Leslie Loomer

In 1876, the Windsor *Mail* reported that 1816 was a very good year for skating on Long Pond and on the Devil's Punch Bowl, back of the college, and by then the boys were playing hurley-on-ice there too. In nearby Halifax and Dartmouth, throughout the 1800s, skaters frequented the North West Arm, the Dartmouth lakes, and a host of other ponds and harbour inlets in and around the city. The Halifax newspapers of that era record that soon after hurley began in Windsor, it was being played on the neighbouring Halifax-Dartmouth ice surfaces as well.

SKATING ON THE NORTH WEST ARM, HALIFAX, LATE 1800s — **Hurley and hockey games were played on the Arm as well.**

PANS

Anyone for Hockey

Newspaper accounts referred to games being played by the military and by teams of local players as well as sailors from visiting British Navy ships. Both men and boys engaged each other in games, side

by side on frozen ponds, lakes, and inlets. Accounts related by early participants later in life verify that the Mi'kmaq played with other teams as well. "Alchamadajk" was the Mi'kmaq term for hurley-on-ice.

New Names for the Game

In 1829, a reporter for the *Colonial Patriot* in Pictou referred to the game of hurley as "break-shins" and told of it being played there as well. By 1831, a Halifax newspaper, the *Nova Scotian*, was reporting news of skating parties being held on the North West Arm and the fact that the game of "wicket" was being played there. The *Colonial Patriot* noted, in 1833, that hurley was being played with great enthusiasm by coal miners in Pictou. News of the new game was spreading and people were trying their hand at it. Hurley-on-ice was catching on. And, in 1842, the Halifax *Morning Post* reported that "ricket" was being played on the Dartmouth lakes.

KING'S COLLEGE CRICKET CLUB, 1907 — The students at King's also played rugby and cricket. Cricket pads were used as "goalie pads" until specially designed ice hockey goalie pads appeared on the market in the early 1900s.

King's-Edgehill School

Other Games Tried

It seems that Nova Scotians tried everything on ice. The English and Scottish members of the military at Windsor and Halifax were familiar with the games of cricket and field hockey as well, and accounts in newspapers show that both were tried on ice in the mid-1800s. Cricket was introduced to Windsor in the 1840s by Charles Bowman, who returned from studies in England, bringing cricket equipment with him. The King's College Three Elms Cricket Club was visited annually by garrison teams from Halifax. They frequently came to Windsor to play cricket, often accompanied by their military band. The influence of cricket on the developing game of hurley-on-ice is evident in the use of the word "ricket," which is a cricket term that defines the goal.

Long Shots Never Scored

In the playing of their particular game, the Mi'kmaq placed their goal stones in line with the direction of play, which prevented scoring by long shots. It appears that this aspect of their game (Oochamkunutk) was adopted by others in the evolution of ice hockey. Nova Scotians played with rocks frozen to the ice in that position (parallel to the sides of the ice surface) for many years.

Lacrosse Abandoned

In 1867, Montreal and Toronto were vigorously promoting lacrosse as Canada's national game. Organizers were sent to the Maritimes and to Great Britain, and the Indian game was typically tried on ice in Halifax. But, as was the case with the members of the Montreal

STOCK SKATE AND BOOT WITH GIMLET — **The gimlet was required to make a hole in the heel to accept the screw extending from the stock (block).**

Garth Vaughan

Football Club who tried lacrosse on ice, it was abandoned in favour of the more popular ice hockey. Each game probably contributed something to the development of ice hockey, although the influence of hurley, from which it originated, remained dominant.

Four Names for the Same Game

References to four types of stickball games, namely hurley, wicket, ricket, and break-shins, were thus appearing in accounts of winter sport in the Windsor-Halifax-Dartmouth and Pictou areas in the very early to mid-1800s. The four activities were essentially different in name only. Eventually, three of the names largely disappeared from use in sports vocabulary, but the term "hurley" remained. By the 1850s, the game of hurley-on-ice was also being called hockey and was gaining recognition in the United States.

Hurley in New Brunswick

The exciting game of hurley or hockey was being played on "stock skates," which were the common type used everywhere. Then a "new and improved" type skate was invented in Nova Scotia that made skating and ice hockey more exciting than ever. In 1865, Starr skates were being worn and enjoyed in the neighbouring province of New Brunswick, and hurley was being played in the Saint John area on Lilly Lake. The records show that boys were proudly using their new Acme self-locking skates.

The Name of the Game, or, Colonel Hockey vs. Hoquet

The reason that the name of the game switched from hurley to hockey, in midstream as it were, is controversial.

Hockey is a centuries-old English word. One derivation of the word "hockey" is founded in the language of the Middle Ages. Hock carts were two-wheeled, horse-drawn carts that were used to transport field crops during the Feast of Harvest Home festivals in the eastern counties of England as early as 1400. A game in which the farm boys got thoroughly covered in mud was played in the fields at festival time, and it was called hockey.

It is quite possible that the English family name, Hockey, was influential in bringing about the change in the name of the game. For many years a story has circulated in the Windsor area that a Colonel Hockey, stationed at the garrison on Fort Edward, had his troops playing the new

> *"HOCKEY" is an English family name which can be found in the phone book in both the Kentville (near Windsor) and Halifax areas of Nova Scotia.*

Nova Scotian game for exercise, and that the game had adopted his name. The name Hockey is to be found in the British Army list located in the Library of Nova Scotia's Legislative Assembly in Halifax. As an example, the records show that quartermaster John Hockey served in the mid-1800s when the game became known as hockey.

A Windsor senior resident, Mr. Leslie Wile, himself a Canadian Army career officer and World War II veteran, tells of the Colonel Hockey referred to in the Windsor story. As a young boy, Leslie worked with his father and grandfather in the woods near Windsor, cutting logs and yellow birch trees for the hockey stick industry. Leslie's grandfather, Nathaniel Conrad, had been an enlisted man in Rudolph's division at the time of the Fenian Raids, and he told Leslie several times that Colonel Hockey was involved in the game and that the game was called "Hockey's game" for some time before it was eventually called hockey.

This oral history, related by Mr. Wile and others, is not documented. Neither is there documentation of the explanation offered by some that the name of the game came from the French word "hoquet," which means a shepherd's crook. Although there is a field game called hoquet that is played in France, I know of no evidence that it was played in Nova Scotia. Nor is there any evidence that ice hockey was ever called hoquet during its developmental years. Ice hockey is a Canadian game which had its origin in the primarily English province of Nova Scotia. Just prior to 1800, when the game began to evolve, the French population had been expelled from the province. The blockhouse on Fort Edward was the headquarters for the officers who carried out the orders for the expulsion. The ships which carried the Acadians away from the area were dispatched from the Avon River below the fort. When the French were gone, the English even changed the name of the town from the French Piziguit to the English Windsor. All of this makes it more unlikely that a French word "hoquet" would be used to name the game that began amongst English, Scottish, Irish, and American settlers. The word "hockey" has a definite English derivation, and there appears to be no plausible reason why Nova Scotians in the mid-1800s would choose a French word to name their new ice game. Add to that the fact that the English already had a field game that they called field hockey, and the possibility of a French derivation for the name of the ice game becomes even more remote.

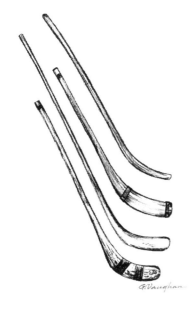

HURLEYS AND HOCKEYS — **From top to bottom, these drawings represent: handmade hurley, c. 1700; Irish regulation hurley, c. 1800; Windsor hockey, handmade, c. 1889; hockey used in RMC - Queens game, 1886.**

Garth Vaughan

Sticks and Stones

Equipment was simple and basic in the early 1800s and remained so for decades. The boys used hurley sticks which they called "hurleys." The shape of their sticks remained the same for many years. Even when ice hockey was first played in the provinces of Quebec and Ontario, seven and eight decades later, little change had taken place. As time went on, the handle length and the blade thickness and shape were gradually altered.

A New Name for the Stick

Just as it was common practice for a hurley player to call his stick a hurley so it became common for hockey players to call their sticks "hockeys." This trend continued on in Nova Scotia at least into the 1940s and those of us who called our sticks hockeys then, still do!

Rickets

The rocks, or "rickets," placed parallel to the sides of the playing surface, frozen to the ice, and used to mark the goal, remained the same until 1890, when they were replaced with metal posts, four feet tall, and positioned parallel to the ends of the ice surface. Net was added to the posts still later, at the turn of the century, to facilitate the job of the goal judge.

"RICKETS" WERE ROCKS — They were used to mark the goalmouth in the early days of ice hockey, just as these concrete blocks were used in 1995.

Garth Vaughan

SAM SLICK HOTEL —
An advertisement that appeared in the local press at the turn of the century. Edward VII was Prince of Wales at the time of his visit to Windsor in 1860.

Windsor Tribune

> *"[In 1863,] ten months after her marriage, the Princess of Wales rose abruptly from watching her husband play ice hockey and rushed home and delivered a son."*
>
> Robert K. Maffey – The Dreadnaught

The Ball Must Go

A ball is essentially unmanageable on ice, and the boys soon replaced it with a wooden disc or puck, at least by the mid-1800s, and probably much earlier. Wooden pucks remained popular for decades and were used in Montreal's first games in the 1870s.

The Rules of the Game

During the decades that hurley-on-ice was developing into ice hockey, roads were scarce and often impassable, and communication between towns was infrequent. Little in the country had been standardized, including the words of the English language; consequently there was little need to standardize the rules of a new game. Since there were no leagues or teams travelling to play in other places, the rules in Windsor could vary from those in Halifax or Pictou and it wouldn't matter. Common rules and regulations were a subject for a future time. Distant interprovincial travel by competing teams didn't occur until the Dartmouth Chebuctos arranged to play teams in Montreal and Quebec and took off on the old Intercolonial Railway in February 1889 for the tournament. It was only then that

rules came into conflict and created a real need for standardization. Even so, like the game itself, rules have continued to change, and new ones have been added from time to time over the years.

I SAY, OLD CHAP, WOULD YOU MIND PASSING THE PUCK? — Bandy is an English ice game which differs somewhat from ice hockey. This photo illustrates the costume worn by players in 1908.

The Book of Winter Sports (1908)

Condemned by the Church

Hockey is very popular all over the world today. However, in its formative stage it was not accepted, let alone appreciated.

Skaters disliked the new ice game. Some people felt it was dangerous and should be forbidden. The clergy condemned it from the pulpit and referred to it as a "desecration of the Sabbath." Ministers preached against it and fought to have it forbidden, especially on Sundays, because the "usual business of church going was not adhered to."

The boys thought it was all right and spent countless hours chasing a ball, a lump of coal, a frozen potato, or a frozen horse bun around the ice with their friends, all the while improving their skating skills and stickhandling ability.

Imagine the dilemma! Parents, at a time when there was little else to do on the Sabbath, had previously had little problem getting the boys to go to church. But the young boys had discovered the thrills of this new winter game and, realizing the shortness of the season, wanted to play every available moment.

"The Dragon" Appears

In the 1860s, hockey players were kept off ponds in order to protect skaters. The man hired to do the dirty job on the ponds in the Halifax area was commonly referred to as "the Dragon," and he was much feared by the energetic youth who had to second-guess his whereabouts in order to find a place to pursue their new winter pastime while the fancy skaters pursued theirs.

Spring Ends the Season

So exciting was hockey for the youth of the province that they hated to see spring approaching, with the inevitable melt and break-up of the natural ice surfaces which had served them so well all winter long. They fought it to the bitter end and skated on wet surfaces well beyond the date when they should have given up. Coming home to supper with heavy melton-cloth pants and home-knit woollen socks and mitts drenched with the water from a melting pond was a common occurrence for the wonder-struck young Nova Scotian players of the day.

CHAPTER 3

The Puck Starts Here

Windsor, Nova Scotia, was settled as early as 1684 and is one of Canada's oldest towns. Over the years the citizens of Windsor have played an important role in the history of our nation and in the development of our national winter sport.

The Acadians

Windsor's first white settlers were Acadian families from Les Mines, which is now the village of Hortonville, on Minas Basin in the Annapolis Valley. At the time, Windsor was known as Piziguit, the French interpretation of "Pesegitk," a Mi'kmaq name which means "the meeting of the waters." It signifies the junction of the Avon and Saint Croix rivers. The Acadians and the Natives were friendly with one another. Acadian farmers prospered as they developed the rich

FORT EDWARD BUILDINGS, WINDSOR — The garrison on Fort Edward, built high above the town in 1870, guarded the townspeople from harm in times of strife and ushered in an era of security, culture, and learning.

Postcard, Valentine and Sons

Fort Edward Buildings, Windsor, N.S.

land along the river banks. When the English began to settle the area as well, strife soon developed between the English on one side and the French and Mi'kmaq on the other.

Fort Edward and the Blockhouse

The English, a military force with a garrison already established at nearby Halifax, built Fort Edward, a blockhouse and garrison on a hill overlooking the town of Windsor, to protect themselves from raids by the French and Mi'kmaq. The blockhouse, a present-day tourist attraction, is the oldest remaining wooden blockhouse in Canada.

The British Takeover

Halifax and Windsor, both being British garrison towns, had the military travelling back and forth, making plans to exert control over the Natives and the Acadians, many of whom were taken prisoner. The women were forced to work at the garrison. The men were put to work improving the road between Halifax and Windsor. The military gradually gained control, and Windsor became predominantly British.

Four Ships from Windsor

The military carried out orders to expel upwards of 5000 Acadians who lived in the area. In 1755, more than a thousand Acadians were rounded up in and around Windsor and placed aboard four ships which sailed from the Avon River, bound for New England. Others sailed from nearby Grand Pré.

The English farmers were protected by the troops at Fort Edward, and they settled along the fertile banks of the Avon where the Acadians had built dykes and cultivated the land. Wealthy and influential politicians and merchants from Halifax were given grants of choice land both in and around the town following the expulsion of the Acadians. They built homes and also established businesses in the area.

Affluent Haligonians visited their Windsor homes in summer and on holidays. Their farms were operated by tenant farmers.

Come to the Fair

Following the expulsion of the Acadians in 1755, American immigrants, known as the New England Planters, arrived in 1760-1761 and, three years later, changed the name of the town from Piziguit to Windsor, in honour of Windsor-on-Thames in England. Along with more English and Irish immigrants, they continued developing and improving the yields from the fertile fields. Regular and busy farm markets were created, which led to the founding of the earliest continuing agricultural fair in Canada, on Fort Edward, in 1765. This was natural, considering the degree of agricultural development of the area and the fact that Nova Scotia was the first province to be developed in the country.

Horse Racing at the Fair

Horse racing, the first in English Canada, was established at the first fair and provided the town with another tourist attraction. The racetrack at the foot of Fort Edward was built on the instructions of the governor of the province. In winter the horse racing moved from Fort Edward to the ice of neighbouring lakes, thus allowing visiting Haligonians to enjoy it the year round.

Churches and Immigration

By 1767 the town had its first public school, and, in 1771, an Anglican chapel was built and other churches followed.

At the beginning of the American Revolution in 1776, United Empire Loyalists moved to the Windsor area along with new immigrants from England and Ireland, and it wasn't long before the Irish Club was organized for dancing, card playing, music, and general entertainment.

COLLEGIATE SCHOOL, WINDSOR, N. S.

King's College School — Founded in 1788 on a 69-acre lot of beautiful rolling pastoral land, purchased for £150 ($600) from a landowner named John Clarke, King's College was Canada's first college.

Canada's First College

In 1788, an Anglican Church school for boys was founded. King's College School served to prepare boys from Windsor, Halifax, and other areas of the Maritimes for college. The following year, King's College, Canada's first college, was established in association with the school. The college was staffed with professors from Cambridge and Oxford, Glasgow, and Queen's College, Galway. Having a college in the country meant that the youth of the area would not have to travel to the United Kingdom for a college education.

By 1791 the townspeople had founded the Windsor Reading Society and a public library, and churches of various denominations were becoming established.

Windsor remained a college town for 135 years. In 1920, a fire burned the main college building, and in 1923 the college was rebuilt in Halifax. However, King's College School, now King's-Edgehill School, remains active in its magnificent setting above the rolling farmland surrounding Windsor.

The "Playground of Halifax"

Windsor had much to offer as a place of interest and beauty, and it had also become a centre of culture and learning. One journalist referred to the town as the "Athens of Nova Scotia." A state of interdependence existed between Halifax and Windsor. There were more good reasons for Haligonians to visit Windsor than there were for Windsorians to go to the city. The gentry of Halifax preferred to have their children educated at King's College School and King's College, where they could visit them, enjoy the atmosphere of the town, and relax away from the noise and confusion of city life. Hunting and fishing in the area were excellent and provided entertainment for the military as well as Haligonians. The town was secure beneath Fort Edward. Because of the close relationship that existed between Halifax and Windsor, one could not really consider them separately. Windsor had become the "Playground of Halifax."

OLD FASHIONED PONY-PHAETON.

PANS

Stagecoach and Hotels

Halifax was reaching out to Windsor and the lands beyond in the Annapolis Valley. In 1816, the first stagecoach line in the Maritimes was established between Halifax and Windsor to accommodate the travelling military and others who wished to visit their children at the college or travel to their country homes. The Avon Hotel, built

HOTEL DUFFERIN — Large hotels like the Avon, Victoria, and Dufferin were situated in close proximity to the railway station. They accommodated many Haligonians who arrived on the Halifax-Windsor Railway as visitors to Windsor, the Playground of Halifax.

WHHSM

AVON BRIDGE — It was completed and open for public travelling on December 1, 1836.

PANS

in 1820, accommodated travellers who had to wait overnight to cross the river on a ferryboat at high tide the next day before they could continue their journey to the Annapolis Valley.

Ye Olde Covered Bridge

The Windsor area was a great source of nourishing food for the people in the Halifax-Dartmouth area. Access to Fort Edward, King's College, and country estates, along with the need for agricultural products, led to the improvement of the road connecting the city to Windsor. This in turn increased access to the fertile lands further on in the Annapolis Valley.

LOW TIDE AND HIGH TIDE, BAY OF FUNDY — Wooden ships lined the wharves of Windsor's busy waterfront in the 1800s. They sailed and arrived in accord with the movement of the world's highest tides.

WHHSM

The longest covered bridge ever built in the province crossed the Avon River in 1836, so the Falmouth-Windsor folk no longer had to get their horses and wagons stuck in the riverbed while crossing at low tide. At a tollhouse on the Windsor side, the keeper collected two cents a crossing for individuals and 25 cents for wagons and passengers. Stage-coach travel was then possible across the province. With the building of the bridge, Windsor became the gateway to the Annapolis Valley.

Ship-Black Watch Windsor - 1877

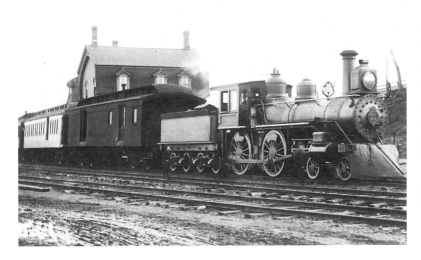

THE SHIP *BLACK WATCH*, WINDSOR, 1877 — Three- and four-masted ships were built on the shores of the Avon River in Windsor and surrounding communities in the 1800s. A renowned port of registry and centre of wooden ship building in the mid-1800s, the town contributed greatly to the building of our nation and to the development of our great national winter game, ice hockey.

WHHSM

Wooden Ships Galore

The shipping of gypsum, lumber, and apples by sea to New England was the stimulus for Windsor to develop into a major shipbuilding centre. By 1840, the town was one of Canada's largest seaports and a world-renowned port of registry, second in traffic only to Montreal and Saint John, with ships visiting from all over the world. The Avon River has the highest tides in the world, and its shores became lined

THE HALIFAX-WINDSOR RAILWAY, 1853 — Nova Scotia's first railway train and station at Windsor.

PANS

ARRIVAL OF GOVERNOR GENERAL, 1896 — Canada's Governor General visited Windsor in 1896, and the citizens turned out in their finery to enjoy the festivities. The town was a picture, with its beautiful Victorian buildings and palatial homes. The following year, Windsor was effectively destroyed by a fire. Within three years it was rebuilt, and Windsorians began their "second period" of growth, as did ice hockey, which had its beginning there a century earlier.

Charles Townsend

with wharves and tall ships at Windsor as well as nearby Hantsport, Mount Denson, Avondale, and the Noel Shore. Wooden ships were being built by the score: schooners, brigs and brigantines, barques and barquentines. Ships built in Windsor, manned by local crew members, sailed to ports around the globe transporting Hants County products.

A Train Bridge Over the River Avon

Businesses had become established and flourished after the Windsor-Halifax Railway was built in 1857. This first public railway in the province gave Halifax better access to Windsor and the Annapolis Valley. With the construction in 1869 of an iron bridge for trains across the Avon River, the new Windsor-Annapolis (W-A) Railway connected other Bay of Fundy communities with Halifax. Access to American markets via the shipping lanes from Windsor was also thus established. The economic boom continued until sail-powered wooden ships gave way to iron steamships built elsewhere, and, in 1890, the wooden ship industry came to a gradual halt.

Sam Slick's House, Windsor, N.S.

The Origin of Ice Hockey

The earliest known reference to hurley being played on ice comes from Thomas Chandler Haliburton, who described it being played on Windsor's Long Pond, around 1800, by boys from King's College School.

At that time there were four groups of young men in the Windsor area who could possibly become involved in a group sporting activity: the students at King's College School and King's College, the military at Fort Edward, the male population of the town, and the Natives. King's was the only college in the entire country at that time where a group of energetic sports-craving boys could be found in a scholastic environment conducive to group recreation. Fort Edward, with its English and Scottish troops, was one of the country's first military establishments, and the energetic young soldiers were likely to become involved in group sport. Otherwise the population of the town consisted of immigrants from Ireland, England, and New England who were busy making a living for their families and not so likely to become involved. The Mi'kmaq were transient, moving from one encampment to another in search of food, and their relationship with others was still not settled.

Each nationality represented in Windsor had its own particular type of field game, including Scottish shinny, English bandy and cricket, Irish hurley, and the Mi'kmaq game called Oochamkunutk. It is probable that all of them exerted some influence on the evolving game of ice hockey. The *Dictionary of the Language of the Mi'kmaq* refers to Oochamkunutk, but references to that game do not appear in Nova Scotia's newspapers in conjunction with the evolution of ice hockey. Neither is bandy referred to. Shinny is mentioned only in passing. Cricket was played early on, in both Halifax

THOMAS CHANDLER HALIBURTON —
Haliburton, noted Canadian author,
wrote the first history of Nova
Scotia and recorded evidence of
hurley being played on ice in
Windsor as early as 1800. Ice
hockey developed from hurley-
on-ice in Nova Scotia.

PANS

Windsor, Nova Scotia

An Outstanding Canadian Town

Settled In 1684

One of the oldest settlements on the American Continent.

Trading Post and British Fort	— Fort Edward, built in 1750
Site of Expulsion of Acadians	— Four ships deported 1000 Acadians, 1755
Home of the Country Fair	— First agricultural fair in Canada, 1765
Site of Canada's First College	— King's College, founded in 1788
Home of Thomas Chandler Haliburton	— First Canadian writer acclaimed internationally, 1796-1865
Birthplace of Hockey	— Began with boys of King's College School at Long Pond, c.1800
First Stagecoach Line in Maritimes	— Halifax to Windsor, 1816
Longest Covered Bridge in Nova Scotia	— Falmouth to Windsor, 1836
Home of Sam Slick	— Created by T. C. Haliburton in *The Clockmaker*, 1836
Gateway to the Annapolis Valley	— Bridge connected Halifax with Annapolis Valley towns, 1836
First Public Railway in Nova Scotia	— Halifax to Windsor Railway, 1853
World Renowned Port of Registry and Shipbuilding Centre	— 1836-1890, when sail gave way to steam
The World's Highest Tides	— 30 to 60 feet in Minas Basin on the Bay of Fundy
Pumpkin Capital of the World	— "Dill's Atlantic Giant Pumpkin," 1979

and Windsor, and doubtless influenced the evolving game. The name hurley was used to describe Nova Scotia's new game on ice for six decades until the game finally took on the form that branded it as Canada's own national winter sport. The two names, hurley and hockey, shared first-place honours for at least a decade, before the name ice hockey took over for good, and even after that hurley was sometimes used as a reference to ice hockey.

With its many ponds adjacent to King's College and Fort Edward, and skating already well established in this town of firsts, Windsor was an ideal place to develop a winter group sport like hurley-on-ice. The school and college students, as well as the soldiers, were the kind of people who were needed to keep it going and to develop the game to its full potential. Their contacts with other towns in the Maritimes and other parts of the country, as well as the United Kingdom and New England, proved to be influential in the spread of the game from its place of origin on Long Pond.

HON. THOMAS CHANDLER HALIBURTON — **Shown as a Judge of the Supreme Court, 1841.**

PANS

SAM SLICK'S WISE SAWS

"Don't look a gift horse in the mouth."

"A stitch in time saves nine."

"Seeing is believing."

"Quick as a wink."

"The early bird gets the worm."

"Truth is stranger than fiction"

T.C. Haliburton

HALIBURTON TOLD THE STORY — Who better to consult regarding the origin of ice hockey in Canada than Tom Haliburton, who witnessed the game in its infancy. Born in Windsor, in 1796, Thomas Chandler Haliburton attended King's College School in early childhood and matriculated at age 14 in 1810. He then continued on at King's College in Windsor and graduated with a degree in law in 1815, following which he studied for a master's degree. Haliburton maintained a close connection with the school and college for 60 of his 69 years. Known by his school friends as Tom, he became a lawyer, judge, Member of the Provincial Legislative Assembly, and a writer of note. He wrote the first history of Nova Scotia, is North America's most quoted author, and is regarded by some as the father of American humour. He specialized in political satire and created Sam Slick, a country clock maker and peddler who became known for his many wise sayings. On moving to England in later life, Haliburton won a seat in the House of Commons. He retired from politics in 1865 and died a few months later. In a four-volume book entitled The Attaché, or, Sam Slick in England *(London, 1844), Haliburton has Sam Slick recall "you boys let out racin', yelpin', hollerin' and whoopin' like mad with pleasure, and the playground, with games at base in the fields, or hurley on the long pond on the ice, or campin' out a-night at Chester lakes to fish."*

This description of hurley-on-ice is the earliest known reference to a stickball game being played on ice in Canada. And since hurley-on-ice went on to develop into ice hockey, Haliburton's comment is of great historical significance.

The Decline and Revival of Windsor

In the mid-1800s, Nova Scotia was Canada's wealthiest province, and Windsor was one of its busiest and most outstanding towns. Enrolment at King's increased steadily, and hurley-on-ice continued to be the chief winter activity for the sports-minded students. In the 1890s the town lost its shipbuilding industry, and many people were out of work. Then, on October 17, 1897, a disastrous fire all but levelled the town. Many of the records of Hants County, of which Windsor was the shiretown, were lost. Windsor's age of glory was over. Although the destruction wrought by the fire was devastating to the townspeople, they rose to the challenge and made plans to clean up the mess and rebuild. All of a sudden, the town became a beehive of activity. There was work for the unemployed and everybody had plenty to do.

WINDSOR, DESTROYED BY FIRE, OCT. 17, 1897 — A lonely looking figure sits viewing the remains of the town in the wake of the fire. The brick chimneys, stone basements, and scorched trees are clearly visible.

Wesley Livingstone

WINDSOR'S AGE OF GLORY ENDED — On a windy Sunday morning, October 17, 1897, townspeople view the remains of their beautiful town.

PANS

The "Second Period" in Windsor

The garrison at Fort Edward and King's College, on the periphery of the town, were spared in the fire. By 1900, the town had largely been rebuilt, and the new look included a new spruce-shingled covered rink. The town, revitalized and looking fresh, was prepared to start life anew.

Ice hockey had gotten its start in Windsor, and the game had steadily grown more popular. In the 1880s and 1890s, a succession of senior teams had competed for local supremacy and played exhibition games with teams of nearby Hantsport, Wolfville, and Halifax.

On its second time around, Windsor was ready to play hockey once again. The town joined with the country's other communities to participate in the growth of the game. In 1900, the year that reconstruction was completed, Windsor had a town league with four senior teams. The Avonians, the Elgraves, the Resolutes, and King's College competed for the Citizens' Trophy, which was donated by the townspeople who filled the rink to capacity in support of their favourite teams.

Windsor's hockey teams consistently won Regional, Provincial, and Maritime Senior Hockey Championships. The town went on to export hockey players to the American Hockey League, Britain, and the NHL. Eventually the town developed the Allan Cup-challenging Windsor Maple Leafs, a team hailed by sports writers as the best senior hockey team in the history of the Maritimes.

A review of Windsor's history leads us to conclude that the small town, where the country's national winter sport had its beginning, was well suited to its role. Furthermore, once the momentum started to build, the game developed and flourished in the town of its beginning as it did elsewhere.

SPREADING THE WORD — Students who attended King's College came from near and far. While most came from Windsor, Annapolis, and Halifax, as well as Saint John, New Brunswick, others came from other parts of the Maritimes and Ontario, as well as England, Scotland, Ireland, the United States, and Spain.

Taking the Game to Others

Windsor, Canada's first centre of culture and learning, produced educated men who went far and wide, teaching others what they had learned at the country's first college. At the same time, they spread the knowledge and skills of the new winter game that began on Long Pond. In taking the game to others, they initiated its spread from coast to coast. The small town where it all began also became an example of courage, excellence of performance, and achievement in the playing of the game. These were standards that could well serve as a model for any community.

THOMAS H. RADDALL, noted Nova Scotia historian and novelist, wrote: "When the soldiers were transferred to military posts along the St. Lawrence and the Great Lakes, they took the game with them, and for some time afterwards continued to send to the Dartmouth Indians for the necessary sticks."

KING'S COLLEGE HOCKEY TEAM, 1921 — Although the Boston press was the first to print evidence that "hockey" was being played in Nova Scotia, it wasn't until 1921 that a Windsor team played in "Beantown." The King's College Hockey Team travelled from Windsor to Boston to play exhibition games with Boston Tech and Harvard, and thence to New Hampshire to play Dartmouth College. Note "Cy" Smith in the centre of the back row.

H. CARLETON "CY" SMITH — "Yarning" about the old days, Cy describes the details of his historic hockey trip to Boston in 1921. Cy was a high scoring forward with King's College and, later, Dalhousie University in the early 1920s.

Garth Vaughan

KING'S COLLEGE HOCKEY SQUAD

Here are the opponents of the Tech hockey team Friday night and Harvard Saturday night. It is a photo of the King's College hockey squad of Windsor, N.S. Top row, left to right — J.A. Ruggles, H.W. Hickman, C.H. Smith, A.E. Gabriel, W.B. Morehouse, manager. Middle row — K.P. Harris, A.A. Dunlop, Captain R. Parnell, T.H. Winter, R.R. Gilbert. Bottom row — M.A. Ross, G. White and E.R. Moulton.

KING'S HOCKEY MEN AT ARENA
Canadians Have Workout on Indoor Surface

The first practice yesterday noon of the King's College town of Windsor, N.S., at the Arena indicated that Tech is in for an interesting session in the game tomorrow night. The Canadians are good skaters, clever stickhandlers and effective team workers. Coach Frank Condon, former crack pro forward, had his King's players at the rink last night to watch Tech and Harvard practice. The coach expressed great surprise at the fine looking squad Harvard had to work with.

King's and Tech will play six men hockey tomorrow night and Harvard will play a seven men game against the Canadians Saturday night. Coaches Claflin and Condon held a conference last night and they agreed on three 15-minute periods. They also agreed on Fred Rocque for one official, and the other man will be selected today. Since Ernie Doody is a native of Halifax, N.S., and is well known by the King's men, his name will be submitted today.

CHAPTER 4

Ice Hockey Heads West

Organized Hockey — Montreal vs. Nova Scotia

It has been said that organized hockey began in Montreal in 1875. While there is no doubt that the game of ice hockey became more organized once James George Aylwin Creighton took it to Montreal, it wasn't exactly in total disarray in Nova Scotia before that time. Those playing the game for the previous seven decades had wooden pucks, Mi'kmaq hockey sticks, Starr skates, and Halifax Hockey Club Rules to guide them. Exhibition games were being played by townspeople, the military troops and officers, and the Mi'kmaq in the Windsor-Halifax-Dartmouth-Pictou-New Glasgow areas of Nova Scotia and in the Saint John, N.B., area, long before it was practised and played elsewhere. Nova Scotia's game of ice hockey gained recognition in the USA 15 years before it was taken to Montreal. The organizational boost the game got in Montreal did not help much in the speed of the spread of the game. It was a full five years from the time the game was played in Montreal until it reached nearby Quebec City in 1880 and another six years before it was played at the colleges in Kingston in 1886. It had taken three-quarters of a century for the game to reach the province of Quebec from Nova Scotia, and it took nearly another quarter century to become established in British Columbia. Neither part of the trip west was exactly speedy.

> *ICE HOCKEY WAS SLOW TO SPREAD*
>
> *Nova Scotia – 1800*
> *Boston – 1859*
> *Saint John, N.B. – 1865*
> *Montreal – 1875*
> *Quebec City – 1880*
> *Ottawa – 1884*
> *Kingston – 1886*
> *Toronto – 1887*
> *Winnipeg – 1890*
> *Victoria – 1890*

Playing "Hockey" in Nova Scotia

The Boston *Evening Gazette*, Saturday edition, November 5, 1859, made it known to the world that there was a new winter sport in Nova Scotia called hockey. "Winter Sports In Nova Scotia" appeared

THE BOSTON *EVENING GAZETTE* — On Saturday, November 5, 1859, an article entitled "Winter Sports in Nova Scotia" described "hockey" being played in Nova Scotia. The editor said he had sent to Halifax for sticks intended to be used to introduce the game to New England.

WINTER SPORTS IN NOVA SCOTIA
WRITTEN FOR THE GAZETTE

In Nova Scotia the time for ice is during the months of December, January and February. The lakes are then frozen and the ground generally covered with snow, although but seldom is there snow enough before Christmas to make sleighing. Skating is the favourite pastime during December, and, indeed, all through the winter, if — as is sometimes the case — there has been a great deal of snow.

There are some excellent skaters in this Province, particularly in Halifax. I have seen young men who could cut their names in German text, or write the Lord's Prayer with skates on the ice easier than most skaters could cut the "outside edges." I don't like to be uncharitable, but I have known some skaters who, I think, would not be able to do it without a written or printed copy before their eyes. Throwing a somersault on skates is almost an impossibility yet I have seen it done successfully.

Fancy skating is not so much practiced in Nova Scotia now as formerly; more attention is paid to games on the ice. Ricket* is the favourite pastime and is played thus: Two rickets are formed at about the same distance, one from the other, that cricketers place their wickets. If there are many players, the rickets are farther apart. A ricket consists of two stones about as large as the cobblestones with which many of our streets have been lately paved — placed about three or four feet apart and frozen to the ice. Teams are then formed by two persons — one opposed to the other — choosing or drawing lots for first choices of partners. The one who claims the first choice selects one from the crowd, the other party then chooses another, and so on alternately until a sufficient number is established for each side. Any number can play the game, and generally, the "more the merrier." Each ricketer is provided with a hurley (or hockey, as it is termed here) and all being ready a ball is thrown into the air which is the signal to commence the play, previous to which, however, a ricket is chosen by each side and placed in charge of a man whose duty it is to prevent the ball from passing through. The game may be 10, 15 or 20, or any number agreed upon, the side counting the number first being winners. The counting consists in putting the ball through your adversary's ricket, each time counting one. From the moment the ball touches the ice, at the commencement of the game it must not be taken in the hand until the conclusion, but must be carried or struck about the ice with the hurlies. A good player — and to be a good player he must be a good skater — will take the ball at the point of his hurley and carry it around the pond and through the crowd which surrounds him trying to take it from him; until he works it near his opponent's ricket, and "then comes the tug of war," both sides striving for the mastery. Whenever the ball is put through a ricket a shout "game ho!" resounds from shore to shore and dies away in hundreds of echoes through the hills. Ricket is the most exciting game that is played on the ice . . . .

*It might be well if some of our agile skaters would introduce the game. It would be a fine addition to our winter sports, and give a new zest to the delightful exercise of skating. We have sent down for a set of hurleys preparatory to its introduction. — Eds. Gazette.

on the front page, and gave an enthusiastic account of the sport that was taking over from ice skating as the most popular winter activity in the province.

Somersaults and the Lord's Prayer

The journalist pointed out that in order to be a good player one must be a good skater and seemed satisfied that there were plenty of those in the province at the time. He outlined the skills of Nova Scotia's "skatists," as skaters were then called, saying that he had seen those who "could do a somersault on skates" and those who "could write the Lord's Prayer on ice with their fancy footwork."

Scoring Rickets with Hurleys

He went on to describe the goalkeeper as "a man whose duty it is to keep the ball from passing through." He said the goal was then called the "ricket" and was designated by two stones the size of cobblestones, placed three to four feet apart and frozen to the ice. Each player was provided with a hurley or hockey stick (interchangeable terms), and, whenever a goal was scored, the players shouted, "Game ho," a cry which the journalist said "resounds from shore to shore and dies away in hundreds of echoes through the hills." Finally, he described it as "the most exciting game that is played on the ice."

Trying It In Boston

The editor was so enthused about the piece that he added an editorial note stating that he had sent off to Nova Scotia for a set of sticks so that skaters could introduce the game to the Boston area.

World's First Hockey Export

James George Aylwin Creighton has the distinction of being the world's first hockey export and captain of the team that won the first game of organized hockey played in Montreal. Creighton, affectionately known to his many friends in Montreal and Ottawa as "J.G.A.C.," grew up in Halifax where he experienced the thrill of the early part of the evolution of Nova Scotia's new exciting winter game, ice hockey. He was only nine years old in 1859 when Boston announced that hockey was being played in Nova Scotia.

Creighton, a Halifax Boy

William Hudson Creighton and his wife, the former Sarah Albro, who were married in the 1840s and lived at 45 Hollis Street, were J.G.A.C.'s parents. The father was an excellent figure skater and had taken part in ice carnivals at the Halifax Skating Rink, built in 1862.

DR. C. BRUCE FERGUSSON — The Nova Scotia provincial archivist, in 1965, when writing on the birthplace of hockey: "If Halifax Rules were used in the so-called first game of 'true' ice hockey, which was played in 1875, was it not reasonable to infer that those rules were evolved on ice, not solely on paper, in Halifax?"

PANS

In 1940, Mr. J.C. Beauchamp of Montreal, a hockey historian, wrote to Creighton's Limited of Halifax, distributors of Mi'kmaq-made hockey sticks to Upper Canadian hockey clubs: "The making of the first sticks has a most important bearing on the origin and early development of hockey. It may also settle the old controversy as to whether Halifax or Montreal was the birthplace of the game."

Young Creighton attended the Halifax Grammar School and quickly matched his father's skating skills. He became an honour student at Dalhousie University, all the time honing his skills as a figure skater and ever-cognizant of the great hockey fever that was developing around him.

The Young Engineer and Sport

Upon graduation, he began working as an engineer on railway construction in Nova Scotia. He moved to Montreal in 1873 where, at age 23, he worked as an engineer on such exciting projects as the Intercolonial Railway, the Montreal waterfront, and the Lachine Canal. In Montreal, he met new athletic friends and joined them as a member of the Montreal Football Club and the Victoria Skating Rink, where he soon became a judge of figure skating.

Ice Hockey as Training for Football

Creighton was successful in interesting his friends in the new game of ice hockey as a means of keeping in shape over the winter months while waiting to play football again. Up until that time, just as in Halifax, the Montreal skating rink had been reserved for skating only. J.G.A.C. and his football friends were able to gain access to the rink for practice sessions of ice hockey, and they became so enthused about developing their new skills that they even bribed the caretaker to allow them to practice on Sundays. (A deduction might be made that the caretaker had become somewhat smitten with the new game himself!) The learning process went on for two years until the two teams, representing the Montreal Football Club and the Victoria Skating Rink, were ready for a face-off.

Canada's First Indoor Ice Hockey Game

March 3,1875, was the big day that nine skilled football players and nine outstanding skaters gave Montrealers their first public display of ice hockey. This was the very first time in the history of the game that a hockey match was played inside a covered building, where players and spectators alike were protected from the weather. It is interesting to note that the officials in Montreal were lenient enough to allow the game to be played in the magnificent Victoria Rink, for back in Nova Scotia, where the game had evolved for the past seven decades, hockey was still confined to outdoor ice surfaces.

Col. Byron Arthur Weston, of Dartmouth — Col. Weston played hockey on the Dartmouth lakes in the 1860s. He and his friends were often joined by the Mi'kmaq in their games. In 1937, he recalled that they "played with a block of wood," and that "the stones marking the place to score goals were placed at opposite angles to those at present." Weston was later president of the Dartmouth Amateur Athletic Association.

PANS

Rules and Equipment

That first match in Montreal was played according to the Halifax Rules. The two dozen sticks used in the game had been sent to Montreal by Creighton's friends back in Halifax especially for the big occasion and would have been made by the native Mi'kmaq craftsmen of Nova Scotia. In Nova Scotia, large stones frozen to the ice always served to designate the goalmouth. A classy innovation at the first Montreal game was the use of metal posts, in place of the conventional cobblestones. The goal markers in that era were positioned parallel to the sides of the ice surface in the Nova Scotia game, rather than parallel to the ends, as is the practice these days. The

THE GOAL UMPIRE — Goal umpires were essential, easy to find, and just as easy to replace. Here, Nova Scotia hockey historian Howard Dill poses as a goal umpire.

Garth Vaughan

Montrealers changed that as well and had their posts placed parallel to the ends of the rink. Nova Scotians continued to play with goalposts parallel to the sides of the playing surface for more than another decade. The first Montreal game was played with nine players a side, who played the whole game; two 30-minute periods with a 10-minute break. The goalkeeper was required to stand the entire game and used the same type of stick as all the other players.

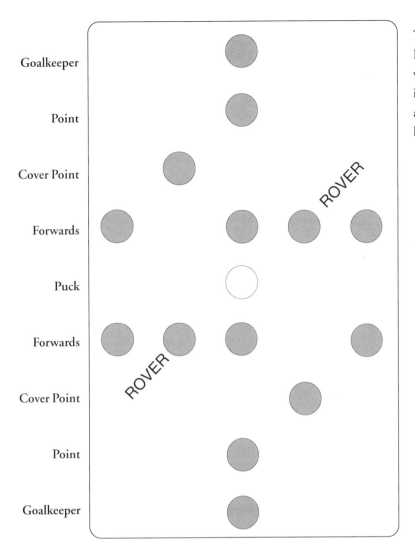

Goalkeeper

Point

Cover Point

Forwards

ROVER

Puck

Forwards

ROVER

Cover Point

Point

Goalkeeper

THE ROVER, POINT, AND COVER POINT — The position of rover was eliminated in 1913, resulting in six-member teams. The point and cover point eventually became known as defence.

The Goal Umpires

In ice hockey these days, the goal judges are positioned safely behind protective glass and press a button whenever the black rubber puck crosses the goal line. It wasn't always that easy, safe, or sure for the decision makers. In the late 1800s, goals were judged by goal umpires. These two gentlemen stood on the ice a little distance from the goal openings, dressed in heavy overcoats, boots, mufflers, and derby hats, watching for the wooden puck to cross the goal line, and signalled by . . . well, since hockey began at a school, and the first officials were probably teachers, what could be more logical to use than a black-handled, loud, brass school bell? If the referee disliked a goal umpire's decision, he would discharge him and choose a replacement from the sidelines.

J.G.A. Creighton, of Halifax —
He is the Father of Organized
Hockey. After he introduced ice
hockey to Montreal from his native
Nova Scotia and helped write
the new Montreal Rules from the
existing Halifax Hockey Club Rules,
he moved to Ottawa. As Law Clerk
of the Senate, he came to know
Arthur and Edward Stanley, sons
of the newly appointed Governor
General of Canada, and other
government personnel.

J.W. "Bill" Fitsell Collection

Score from Either Side or from Behind

In Nova Scotia's game, the goalmouths, being parallel to the sides of the rink, had the advantage of preventing long shots on goal, for the puck would merely bypass the goalmouth. However, the position of the goal markers, along with the absence of a net, meant that players could score on the goalkeeper from either side, and from behind as well, if he didn't turn quickly enough to face the action. (And we think goaltenders are busy today!) The fact that the goalkeeper was not allowed to sit, kneel, or sprawl on the ice made things more difficult for him as well. Of course, one of Nova Scotia's rules worked to the advantage of the goalkeeper in this regard: the puck was not allowed to be lifted off the ice.

Best Skates for Best Hockeyists

News reports made no mention of the skates used by the players, but it is generally conceded that Starr skates, designed and made in Dartmouth, Nova Scotia, were the best available in the world and would be the choice of the players. A very early photo of McGill students playing ice hockey in 1881 shows them using the newer self-fastening Starr skates rather than the older-style stock skates. Play was stopped whenever a player lost a skate or had trouble securing a skate to his boot. No screws were used to attach skates to boots; all skates were held in place with the ingenious spring apparatus which had been devised and patented by the Starr Manufacturing Company of Dartmouth a decade earlier.

A wooden puck cut from a 3-inch-diameter tree limb was the commonly chased object back in Nova Scotia, and likewise the Montrealers used a wooden disc for their first game. (Although vulcanized rubber was available, it was not used as a material for pucks for another decade.)

> HENRY JOSEPH, *a Montreal businessman who played in that city's first hockey game in 1875, said that James George Aylwin Creighton was the "leading spirit" in the introduction of hockey into Montreal and added that he could not recall seeing hockey sticks before that time, nor could he recall evidence of anyone playing hurley or shinny on skates. Finally, Joseph said that "to Creighton should go the credit for the origin of ice hockey in Montreal."*

Read All About It !

Fair play, good skating, and team skill honoured Creighton that day as he captained the winning team, the Montreal Football Club, which beat the Victoria Skating Rink team, 2-1.

The newspaper report of the hockey game between the skaters and the football players indicated that a good deal of rough play was involved, much to the disappointment of some of the ladies, who left the rink in disgust. However, most of the spectators remained and enjoyed the match, and continued to go back for more, as ice hockey became steadily more popular in Montreal that season and every season since.

Halifax Rules

In 1873, when 23-year-old J.G.A. Creighton began introducing his new Montreal sporting friends to Nova Scotia's winter game of ice hockey, he taught them the rules as he knew them. These rules were referred to in Montreal as the Halifax Hockey Club Rules and were used to guide the Montreal teams through their first games of ice hockey. Because the game had been restricted to such a small area of the province of Nova Scotia for three-quarters of a century, and struggled to gain acceptance even there, the rules, known and understood by those playing the game, apparently had not yet been produced in print. The need to do so had not yet been created.

> DR. SANDY YOUNG, *author of* Beyond Heroes *and professor of sports history at Dalhousie University, said in 1988: "The facts lead to one conclusion: While it is true that very primitive forms of hockey-like games are centuries old, the home of Canadian hockey is Nova Scotia. Other claims cannot be supported by the evidence available."*

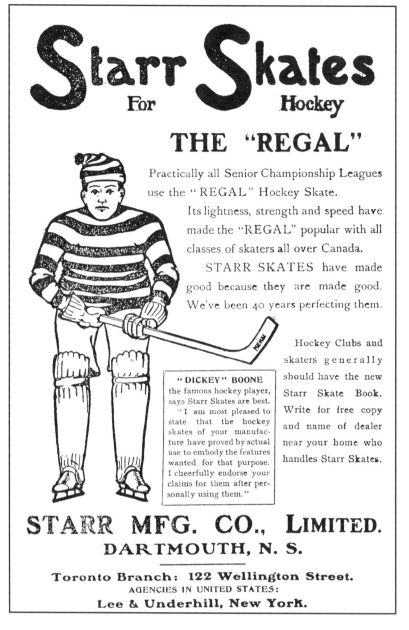

New Rules for the Organized Game

Excitement created by the first Montreal game spread quickly,
leading to the formation of other teams in and about the city.
Creighton's interest in ice hockey continued as he worked with fellow members of the Montreal teams to develop and fine-tune the
game. Meanwhile, Creighton, the athlete and student, decided to
enter McGill University in 1877. He already had an Arts degree
from Dalhousie University and now he was headed for a degree in
Law. A very busy young man, Creighton was also secretary of the
Metropolitan Club, an exclusive Montreal men's club. In that position,
he was involved in the publishing of a new set of rules for ice hockey.

Creighton Not a McGill Player

Four years after Creighton arrived in Montreal, and he and his friends began practising their hockey skills, McGill formed its first hockey team, in 1877. While attending McGill, Creighton did not play on the college team, choosing to lead the top city team called, simply, Montreal. Until that time, all Montreal games had been played according to the Halifax Rules, which Creighton had learned back in his home town. Those rules had not been officially printed, but now, due to the efforts of Creighton and his friends, the world would have its first set of official ice hockey rules. The new rules were a modification of the Halifax Rules, including additions from ground hockey, and would be called the Montreal Rules.

Montreal Rules vs. Halifax Rules

Forward passing, which was permitted under Halifax Rules, was not to be allowed in the new Montreal Rules. The Halifax Hockey Club Rules continued to govern the game in Nova Scotia for years, albeit with minor changes. Meanwhile, the new Montreal Rules guided the further development of the game in Quebec and Ontario.

Five Years from Montreal to Quebec City

Quebec City formed its first hockey club in 1880 and played with Montreal in 1881, six years after the game arrived in Montreal from Nova Scotia. As exciting as the game was to some, it was as slow to spread in the province of Quebec as it had been in the Maritimes. In the 1880s, Quebecers were playing Quebecers and Nova Scotians were playing Nova Scotians. King's College was travelling to Dartmouth to play the Ramblers on the Dartmouth lakes. In Windsor, in the late 1880s, the Alerts, Blue Jackets, Juniors, and King's College were competing with each other and with Acadia College in nearby Wolfville. The Crescents and Wanderers and Dalhousie University of Halifax were playing with the Ramblers and the Chebuctos of Dartmouth. There was lots of ice hockey activity in both Nova Scotia and Quebec, but never had teams from the two areas where ice hockey was developing come together for a tournament.

THE HALIFAX RULES — The Halifax Rules were recorded by James Power, sports writer for the Halifax Herald. Power knew ice hockey in its formative years, and began his reporting career in 1879, when the game was taking hold in Montreal. Following is his 1937 list of rules that governed the game in Nova Scotia in the mid-1800s.

- *The game was played with a block of wood for a puck. The puck was not allowed to leave the ice.*
- *The stones marking the place to score goals were placed on the ice at opposite angles to those at present.*
- *There was to be no slashing.*
- *There was to be no lifting the stick above the shoulder.*
- *When a goal was scored, ends were changed.*
- *Players had to keep on side.*
- *The forward pass was permitted.*
- *Players played the entire game.*
- *There was a no-replacement rule.*
- *The game had two 30 minute periods, with one 10 minute break.*
- *The goalkeeper had to stand for the entire game.*
- *Goals were decided by the goal umpires, who stood at the goalmouth and rang handbell.*

THE DARTMOUTH CHEBUCTOS, **1888** — One of Canada's earliest hockey team photos shows J. Brown (far left) wearing shin pads. This team, organized by the Dartmouth Amateur Athletic Association, appears to have been the first in the country to use shin pads.

J. W. "Bill" Fitsell

JAMES POWER OF HALIFAX — The Dean of Canadian Sports Writers, knew ice hockey before it spread to Montreal.

PANS

Dartmouth Chebuctos Bridge the Gap

Then, in 1889, the progressive and skilful Dartmouth Chebuctos, who had dominated the Halifax Hockey League for several years, made arrangements for a visit to Quebec to play exhibition games with the crack Montreal and Quebec City teams. Travel was by the Intercolonial Railway and would be a tiresome 1200-mile journey and a tense experience for the adventurous young Nova Scotians. The games got some press coverage in Quebec but caused little excitement in Nova Scotia. The Dartmouth players held their own when playing by Halifax Rules, and the Montrealers and Quebecers won when Montreal Rules were followed. It was a wonderful experience for both parties and did much to further the development of ice hockey. A fair exchange took place. The Dartmouth team introduced the forward pass to their counterparts. The Quebec and Montreal teams showed the Nova Scotian solo artists the advantages of team play. The Nova Scotians, who until that time played with goal rocks parallel to the sides of the rink, went home favouring goalposts parallel to the ends of the ice surface. The tournament succeeded in bringing together teams playing by different rules and created the need for standardization. Future interprovincial tournaments would require universal rules. One can only imagine the conversations in the dressing rooms in Quebec and on the train cars on the long trip back to Nova Scotia, for a new stage in the development of Canada's great winter game was about to begin as a result of that historic meeting. And indeed the stage was set for several other radical changes in the way that ice hockey would be played in the future as a result of similar tournaments which were to follow in other provinces.

Dean of Sports Writers to the Rescue

In 1937, James Power of Halifax, labelled by Montreal sports writer and commentator Elmer Fergusson, as "the Dean of Canadian Sports Writers," wrote down the Halifax Rules as they had been commonly understood by participants in Nova Scotia in the formative years of the game. Power began his career as a sports reporter in 1879 and knew people who had played the game long before that time. Fergusson, from Montreal, upset with claims being made in Kingston, Ontario, by Captain James Sutherland regarding the origin of ice hockey, was attempting to clarify the origin of the game. In preparing this list, Power consulted Colonel Byron Weston, who had played hockey in the mid-1800s in Halifax and Dartmouth with men from the garrison and towns, as well as Mi'kmaq players.

Ottawa, Creighton, and the Stanleys

Two years after organizing ice hockey in Montreal, Creighton again entered university and completed his studies at McGill in 1880 with a Bachelor of Law degree. Then, after working for a Montreal law firm for a while, he accepted the position of Law Clerk of the Senate. Leaving his many athletic friends in Montreal behind, he moved to Ottawa and his new position. Ice hockey was becoming popular in Ottawa, as it was spreading toward the West Coast. The new friendships he made in Ottawa included Senators and aides-de-camp, as well as the family of the newly appointed Governor General, Lord Stanley of Preston. Lord Frederick Arthur and Lady Constance Stanley were introduced to ice hockey at the Montreal Winter Carnival shortly after their arrival in Canada in 1888. They had two daughters and eight sons. The girls and two sons came to Canada with their parents and attended the carnival with them. They all fell in love with ice hockey and became very involved. One daughter, Lady Isobel, tried her hand at the game, as did the Governor General himself. The two sons were interested in ice hockey and joined with Creighton and others in forming a hockey team called the Rideau Hall Rebels. Creighton, 38 by then, was still very active in skating and hockey.

THE RIDEAU HALL REBELS IN 1888, LORD STANLEY'S FAVOURITES — "J.G.A."
Creighton of Halifax is the Father of Organized Hockey. After he
introduced ice hockey to Montreal from his native Nova Scotia and helped
write the new Montreal Rules from the existing Halifax Hockey Club Rules,
he moved to Ottawa. As Law Clerk of the Senate, he came to know Arthur
and Edward Stanley, sons of the newly appointed Governor General of
Canada, and other government personnel. Along with John Barron, MP
from Lindsay, senators, aides-de-camp, and the two Stanley boys, Creighton
helped organize the Rebels hockey team. Shown in white with cap and dark
sash, he has Arthur to his right and Edward sitting at his feet. The
Governor General was so taken with the involvement of his sons in Canada's
new game that he was stimulated to present a $48.66 silver rose bowl,
brought from London, England, to be used for amateur hockey
competition. In the photo are, standing: Capt. Wingfield, Arthur Stanley,
Sen. L.G. Power, H.A. Ward, J.S.D. Lemoine; seated: Edward Stanley, J.G.A.
Creighton, A.H. MacMahon, J.A. Barron, H.B. Hawkes.

J.W. "Bill" Fitsell

Borrowing the Stanley Car

Both Arthur and Edward Stanley devoted themselves to the game, much to the satisfaction of their father, who was quite taken with it as well. Lord Stanley, who had just taken up his new post in June, made life much easier for the Rebels by lending the team his personal rail car for their trips to and from Lindsay, Kingston, and Toronto for games over the next few years.

The Stanley Cup: A Bargain at $48.66

Proud of his sons' involvement in the Rebels team and totally excited about the game itself, Lord Stanley wanted to stimulate interest in competition between senior teams in the area. Therefore, in 1893, he had a friend bring a gold-lined silver rose bowl from England to be used as a trophy. At a cost of ten guineas ($48.66 Canadian), it was to become the symbol of excellence for amateur hockey from Halifax to Victoria. Because he so favoured the Rebels team, Lord Stanley dearly wished to see Ottawa be the first to claim the Lord Stanley Challenge Trophy. And the Rebels almost did it. On a real winning streak, beating the teams from Quebec on home ice, they unfortunately succumbed to the powerful Montreal Amateur Athletic Association (MAAA) team, which became the first winner of the now famous trophy. It would be 10 long years before the Ottawa team would win the Stanley Cup. By then Lord Stanley was back in England and never did see his Rebels become champions.

STANLEY CUP WITH ADDED BASE

Canadian Hockey Year Book (1923)

The Stanleys and the Royals

Soon after offering the Lord Stanley Challenge Trophy in 1893, the Governor General's term of office in Canada came to an end and the Stanleys returned to England. Shortly after their arrival there, Lord Stanley and his sons played a game of ice hockey on the grounds of Buckingham Palace with the royal dukes.

The Stanley Cup: Rejected

Since 1893, there have been many interesting stories surrounding the winning of the Stanley Cup, but none more fascinating than the one concerning the first win. Just as hockey itself was a new game, not yet played from coast to coast, so trophies were new. At the time there was a general agreement concerning trophies: that any team good enough to win a championship three years in a row would take permanent possession of the trophy. It seems that this was not to be the case with the new Stanley Cup, and therefore the MAAA players decided that they didn't want it. They did not want the Stanley Cup! Nor would they accept it for another six months. Why should they? They had just won the large and very beautiful trophy of the Canadian Amateur Hockey Association, three years in a row, and they were allowed to keep it. And here was this new Stanley rose bowl, a mere seven and one-half inches tall, which had to be returned each year, with no chance of permanent possession. Following considerable discussion between the trustees of the trophy and the Montreal Amateur Athletic Association executive, it was decided that a ring of silver, containing the names of the winners, would be added to the trophy, along with a black, shiny, wooden base. That seemed to be more acceptable to the players, who then decided in favour of accepting the brand new Stanley Cup.

The World's Most Coveted Ice Hockey Trophy

The Stanley Cup has remained in circulation ever since as a challenge cup. For years it was symbolic of amateur supremacy, and ever since professionalism crept into Canada's great game, it has become the most coveted hockey trophy in the world, even if the Montreal team didn't want it back in 1893.

Early Hockey in Kingston, Ontario, and the Nova Scotia Connection

Kingston's early hockey players not only played with Nova Scotia hockey sticks and Starr skates but also learned how to play the game from a Nova Scotian.

Roderick "Roddy" McColl (Cadet #149), of New Glasgow, is credited with taking hockey to Kingston from Nova Scotia and teaching the RMC students to play. He attended the Royal Military College from 1882 to 1886 and served as goal umpire in the first game of ice hockey played in the Limestone City in 1886. Although the game took place in Kingston, it was a match between the students of the Royal Military College and Queen's University and did not directly involve the townspeople. The students on the two teams, for the most part, were from out of town. The RMC team was stacked with Maritimers from the Halifax-Windsor area and Moncton, N.B., and a goalie from Ottawa, as well as Quebecers. The Queen's team was made up of students from such places as Hamilton, Pembroke, and Ottawa, and they sent to Nova Scotia for

CADET #149, RODERICK "RODDY" McCOLL — This cadet, from New Glasgow, N.S., is credited with teaching his fellow cadets at RMC to play ice hockey and years later said, "The Nova Scotia boys defeated Kingston in hockey."

RMC

JAMES GEORGE AYLWIN CREIGHTON (1850 - 1930): THE FATHER OF ORGANIZED HOCKEY

W.L. Murray, writing in the Montreal Gazette in 1936, gave credit to two McGill students for having originated ice hockey and written the rules by which the game was played. He was proven wrong by Henry Joseph, a McGill student who also played in Montreal's first games along with J.G.A. Creighton of Halifax. Joseph gave credit to Creighton for taking the game, the rules, and the sticks to Montreal. (McGill's first ice hockey team was formed in 1877.)

J.G.A. CREIGHTON

PANS

J.G.A. Creighton is considered by many to be the Father of Organized Hockey, although he is not yet identified among the builders of ice hockey enshrined in Canada's Hockey Hall of Fame. Born in Halifax when ice hockey was in its early stages of development, he became an outstanding figure skater and football player, and learned Nova Scotia's new game when it still had two names, hurley and ice hockey. Moving to Montreal to work as an engineer, he taught new friends to play ice hockey, and was instrumental in turning the game into an organized sport with rules, played inside, with a limited number of players. Creighton captained the winning team in Montreal's first game of ice hockey, on March 3, 1875, played by teams representing the Montreal Football Club and the Victoria Skating Rink. They used Halifax Hockey Club Rules and hockey sticks sent by Creighton's friends from Nova Scotia

for the occasion. Creighton later moved to Ottawa and played a role in the development of ice hockey there just as he had done in Montreal. A member of Ottawa's Rideau Hall Rebels Hockey Club, along with the Governor General's sons Arthur and William Stanley, Creighton helped to popularize ice hockey in Ontario centres. His efforts led to the donation of the Lord Stanley Challenge Trophy, which became the world's most coveted hockey trophy, the Stanley Cup. Creighton was Law Clerk of the Senate and maintained his interest in figure skating and ice hockey until his death in Ottawa in 1930. "J.G.A.C.," as he was commonly referred to by sports writers and friends, is a member of the Nova Scotia Sports Hall of Fame. Perhaps one day the nation will honour him as the Father of Organized Hockey, for in addition to initiating the first game in Montreal, he also captained the winning team.

In April, 1898, Dr. A.H. Beaton, Secretary of the Ontario Hockey Association, wrote in the Canadian Magazine: "Nearly twenty years ago hockey, as a scientific sport, was introduced into Upper Canada from Nova Scotia, the latter being the indisputable home in Canada of this game."

GENERAL ARTHUR GRANT BREMNER — While a student at RMC. Bremner was a forward on the team that first played ice hockey in Kingston, Ontario, in 1886. After graduating from RMC, he had a military career in India and spent his retirement years in the Annapolis Valley of his home province, Nova Scotia.

Frances Bremner

hockey sticks with which to play the game. The principal of Queen's University at the time of their first game was George M. Grant of Stellarton, Nova Scotia. Grant had been the pastor at Saint Matthew's Church in Halifax for some time before he had been called to the Queen's position and would have been able to advise the students on where to acquire sticks.

Limestone City's First Team

At the time of the first public performance by the new college teams in 1886, the citizens of Kingston were still quite unfamiliar with ice hockey, and hockey activity remained confined to the universities for another four years. It was not until 1890 that the boys from the Limestone City formed their first competitive hockey team.

By the time the city of Kingston's first team got organized, hockey activity back east in Nova Scotia was booming, and there were at least ten teams in the Windsor – Dartmouth – Halifax area. The Dartmouth Chebuctos had already been on their first inter-provincial road trip to play teams in both Montreal and Quebec, where hockey was played for a decade before it reached Kingston. The RMC - Queen's games were played according to the Montreal Rules drawn up by Creighton and his Montreal friends.

Kingston's Great Contribution

J.W. "Bill" Fitsell, hockey historian and resident of Kingston, author of *Hockey's Captains, Colonels and Kings*, pointed out in his book that the real significance of the RMC - Queen's games had nothing to do with the origin of hockey as some have indicated, but rather that the games "brought together players from two areas of Canada, Halifax and Montreal, where hockey originated and developed, and also from the two centres where it first spread, Quebec and Ottawa, and produced dedicated players who were dispersed to other non-playing centres throughout North America."

As the RMC - Queen's players went off to teach their hockey skills to friends in other parts of the country, they perpetuated the tradition begun by the boys at King's in Windsor and carried on by J.G.A. Creighton of Halifax, who took hockey from his native Nova Scotia to his new friends in both Montreal and Ottawa, and Cadet Roddy McColl, who had done the same for his new friends in Kingston. By introducing the game to new places, these young Canadian athletes made a major contribution to the spread of our national winter sport from one coast to the other, over a period that lasted nine decades.

"Captain Jim" and the Kingston Myth

Confusion concerning the position of Kingston, Ontario, in the development of ice hockey began as early as 1924, when James "Captain Jim" Sutherland made the unfounded claim that Kingston was the birthplace of hockey. Unfortunately, in making his Kingston claim, he failed to establish the dates that ice hockey had been played in either Nova Scotia or Montreal.

A large, handsome, and popular man, he was a great story-teller and respected hockey executive. Eager reporters printed his message, and the myth became established. His claim went unchallenged for years and was reprinted again and again.

Dates Meaningless to Jim

In 1924, Sutherland claimed, "I think it is generally admitted and has been substantially proven . . . that the actual birthplace of organized hockey is the city of Kingston in the year 1888."

The truth, of course, is that ice hockey had actually been played two years earlier than that date in Kingston, and that it had been played more than 13 years earlier in Montreal, to say nothing about Nova Scotia, where it originated nearly a century before.

Finally, in 1928, Montrealers, having heard the truth misrepresented too often and knowing that the game had been played in their city since 1875, objected to Captain Sutherland's claim.

CAHA Follows the Myth

Again in 1943, as a member of a committee appointed by the Canadian Amateur Hockey Association to study the origin of hockey, Captain Jim and his two friends George Slater and Billy Hewitt (father of veteran hockey broadcaster Foster Hewitt) once again, without sound proof, claimed Kingston to be the birthplace of hockey and published that claim in an official report accepted by the CAHA.

Regan's Lesson, Cope's "Nope!"

This time, two Nova Scotians also objected. A Halifax journalist, John Regan, wrote a letter to Sutherland and offered a history lesson on Nova Scotia. Regan, who had written a book called *First Things In Acadia,* under the nom de plume John Quinpool (Regan lived on Quinpool Road), was very knowledgeable about things which had begun in Canada's oldest province and tried to set the record straight, with little effect. The Kingston myth was well estab-

CAPTAIN JAMES SUTHERLAND, KINGSTON, ONTARIO — Canada's early hockey researchers, James Sutherland, George Slater, and Billy Hewitt, comprised the CAHA committe that studied and presented evidence about the origin of hockey. While these three men each contributed greatly to the development of ice hockey in their own area of the country, they also contributed to the confusion concerning the origin of the sport.

J.W. "Bill" Fitsell

> *"When you hear an opinion, consider the source."*
>
> Anonymous

Royal Military College's Hockey Team 1888 — Standing: E.M. McDougall, H.B.D. Campbell, Arthur G. Bremner, E.A. Whitehead. Seated: A.N.J. Smart, W.A.H. Kerr, W.H. Rose. Note the Starr spring skates leaning against the table. The players were from Nova Scotia, Quebec, and Ottawa. Their first game, played with Queen's University in 1886, took place two years after hockey was introduced at Ottawa and 11 years following the time that it was first played in Montreal. The players used sticks made in Nova Scotia and the team was tutored by a Nova Scotian.

James Bremner

Donald "Dan" Wilson of Halifax who, having received a B.A. degree from Dalhousie, went on to Queen's to study Theology and Journalism, observed in 1886 that the newly formed Queen's hockey team sent to Halifax for hockey sticks that were handmade by the Mi'kmaq of Nova Scotia. (Dan frequently told this story to relatives.)

lished. A much respected elderly Mi'kmaq historian, who had made hockey sticks for the developers of the game, wrote a letter to the editor of the Halifax *Herald* and registered an objection, saying that the game, as well as the sticks, originated in Nova Scotia. Cope's words fell on deaf Ontario ears as well.

Captain Jim Finally Concedes

In later life, when considering the fact that the hockey sticks used in the early games in Montreal and Kingston had come up from Halifax, Captain Jim Sutherland conceded that the Nova Scotia capital preceded most centres in playing the game. "Otherwise, why send to Halifax for sticks?" he asked.

Paying no attention to dates, or to the fact that Captain Jim had finally realized and admitted to his error, some continue to perpetuate the Kingston myth to this day.

George M. Grant, Principal, Queen's University, 1877–1902

George M. Grant was born at Stellarton, Nova Scotia, on December 22, 1835. He was educated at Pictou Academy and Glasgow University, Scotland. From 1863 to 1877 he was pastor of St. Matthew's Church in Halifax. He championed the leading issues of the day: free schools, union of the provinces, and church union among

STARR MANUFACTURING AD — This ad appeared in the *Canadian Illustrated News* in 1872. Starr self-fastening skates clamped onto the soles and heels of boots and they served Canada's pioneer hockeyists from the time they first appeared in 1865 until they were replaced with skates which were attached to boots permanently with small screws, c. 1890.

PANS

E.M. Orlich of Montreal, commenting on the CAHA Committee Report of 1943, which supported the Kingston claim, said "No amount of eye-wash, back-wash, or white-wash can convince any individual, who has seen the evidence in my possession, that Kingston has even the slightest shred of an historical claim, either to the origin of ice hockey, or the proposed Hockey Hall of Fame."

DR. GEORGE M. GRANT — Principal of Queen's University, 1877-1902.

QUA

the Presbyterians. Following a three-month trip from Halifax to Victoria with Sir Sanford Flemming in 1872, he wrote an account of the journey, entitled, *From Coast to Coast*. In 1911, the *British Weekly* said, "Dr. Grant was the first author who understood the tremendous possibilities of Canada, and brought them home to a great public. He was an able and far sighted man, a Canadian through and through, and one of the greatest of Canada's sons. He is destined to hold a permanent place in history."

In 1877, he was appointed principal of Queen's University and held the position for a quarter of a century, until his death in 1902. It was said of Grant that "every public question claimed his attention." It is therefore not unreasonable to assume that he would have been quite aware of ice hockey developing in his native Nova Scotia when he was living and serving in Halifax in the formative years of the game. Grant was probably also quite cognizant of the woodworking skills of the native Mi'kmaq and their ability to make high-quality hockey sticks. Therefore, along with Cadet #149, Roddy McColl of the Royal Military College, he would have known where to find a few good hockeys when the boys of RMC and Queen's finally decided to take up the Nova Scotian winter game in 1886.

Winnipeg and Victoria in 1890

In the 1880s, ice hockey was being played in only three Canadian provinces: Nova Scotia, Quebec, and Ontario. However, once it became popular in Ontario, it spread quickly to the West, and, in 1890, the game was introduced to both Winnipeg and Victoria, thus completing the trans-Canada introductory trip.

Quick Learners

Though Winnipeggers were late in being introduced to the game, they greeted it with enthusiasm and set out to make up for lost time. They formed their first team, called the Victorias, in November,

> *William Kerr of Montreal played for Queen's first hockey team in 1886. In commenting on the hockey sticks imported from Nova Scotia, he said they were "simply wonderful sticks . . . such beauties that they were, made out of small trees, planed down, with roots for blades; warranted irresistible by any shin!" (What Kerr and others did not know was that the sticks were not made in Halifax but rather were handcarved by Mi'kmaq at Tufts Cove, Millbrook, Pictou Landing and the Annapolis Valley.)*

1890, and played their first official games in 1891 with the newly formed Winnipegs. Two years later there were over 30 teams in the city and another in every village and town around it. As in other centres, the game was traditionally brought to the city by men who had learned it in the East. Like those in other provinces, they also played their first games on outdoor ice surfaces. By 1893, the players were not only good, they were also innovative. When an all-star team headed east by train on a tournament that year, the players showed that they had developed a feel for the game. They also introduced their eastern counterparts to their new moves: the wrist shot and the face-off. They also revealed their respect for the goalie, who was allowed to wear cricket pads and use a goal stick. Originally, the puck was required to stay on the ice when it went over the goal line. Then, as lifting became permitted in Montreal, and the wrist shot developed in Winnipeg, it became quickly apparent that the goalie was going to require some special equipment, at last. Cricket pads were just the thing, for the time being.

Jack McCulloch, the "Winnipeg Wonder"

One of the founding members of the Winnipeg Victorias, a speed skater named Jack McCulloch was fond of German-made tube racing skates. Eager to contribute to the developing game of ice hockey, he used the same design, but without the long extension, and fashioned new, lightweight skates for hockey. The year was 1895 when Jack, Canada's speed skating champion and member of the now famous Winnipeg Victorias, developed tube hockey skates for his fellow team-mates. Jack was a partner in a skate manufacturing company, McCulloch and Boswell, which made hockey tube skates for players in the West, while Starr made famous Silver King stainless steel tubular skates in the East.

J.W. "Bill" Fitsell, maintained that Cadet Kerr "gave an important clue to hockey history when he reported that some of the senior cadets remembered that Halifax made 'simply wonderful sticks.'" He also stated: "The three Queen's - RMC matches, 1886-1888, which followed the first Montreal games by a decade, were of historic significance to the new ice sport. They brought together players from two areas of Canada, Halifax and Montreal, where hockey originated and developed, and also from the two centres where it first spread, Quebec and Ottawa, and produced dedicated players who were dispersed to other non-playing centres throughout North America."

J.W. "Bill" Fitsell, Kingston hockey historian, on noting his city's involvement in the origin of hockey, commented: "As a resident of Kingston, Ontario, I must admit it smarts a little to broadcast that this historic Limestone City, despite its early association with the game of shinny and early growth in the new game here, is not the birthplace of hockey as legend claims."

J.W. "Bill" Fitsell

J. W. "Bill" Fitsell

Ice Hockey Spreads Like Prairie Fire

WINNIPEG VICTORIAS, 1893 — They devised the wrist shot and added a piece to the goalkeeper's stick to allow him to handle the shots. The following season, the goalkeeper was allowed to use cricket pads to protect his shins. A wider blade and cricket pads were new for goalies. Previously, they used an ordinary stick and no shin pads. Padded gloves were 11 years away; they appeared on the market in 1904.

PAM

Having found its way to the major centres of the West by 1890, it wasn't long before smaller and more remote places took up the new game as well. Easterners were moving West by the score in the 1880s and 1890s and many of them were responsible for carrying the game with them. Men who had become experts on a team moved on and became organizers of new teams in the west, north and south. University teams began touring by train, playing and introducing the game to Americans, city by city. These college games were exciting and drew larger crowds with each successive visit of the young Canadians. The tradition begun by the young boys at King's College School in Windsor a century before was carrying on, only on a grander scale. It wouldn't be long before both Canadians and the new American players would be carrying ice hockey to other countries around the world.

Canada's Game

The year before ice hockey arrived in Winnipeg, Montreal and Quebec had their first experience with the forward pass introduced by the Chebuctos of Dartmouth, Nova Scotia. Teams were all using the talents of a special type of player, called the rover, which also originated in Nova Scotia. The year that ice hockey began in Winnipeg, the Halifax Hockey League converted from rickets, or rocks, to metal posts as goal markers, having adopted the innovation from Quebec players. It would be another decade before previously bare goalposts were to be covered with fishnet in Halifax, creating the Nova Scotia box net, and thus completing the basic equipment used to play the game: Mi'kmaq hockey sticks, wooden pucks, Starr hockey skates, and box nets.

Many changes were still to take place before the game would be recognizable in its present-day form, but for the time being, the game which started with a group of young boys on the East Coast had been introduced to their counterparts on the West Coast and was appreciated everywhere across our great nation as a new and wonderfully exciting form of winter recreation.

STARR RACING TUBE SKATE — **A lightweight racing tube skate with the STARR trademark in the boot plate was attached to boots with small screws. This skate model appeared at the turn of the century and was immediately popular with speed skaters. Starr also produced a tube hockey skate at the same time.**

Garth Vaughan

Hockey Gets Better and Better

Wherever ice hockey was carried, and taught, significant developments took place in the playing of the game. Halifax and Dartmouth popularized the game that was first played in Windsor and created the stimulus for Starr to develop new and better skates. Then J.G.A.Creighton took ice hockey to Montreal. Montreal took it inside, improved the calibre of play, wrote new rules, furthered its popularity, and spread it to Quebec City and Ottawa. Ottawa further popularized the game and was responsible for the origin of the Stanley Cup. Some players who learned the game in Ottawa and Quebec joined players from the Maritimes at RMC and Queen's and established the game in the university setting. The RMC and Queen's players stimulated the Kingston people to take up ice hockey and carried the game to the east and west and to American universities. Winnipeg quickly developed the quality of the game and went back East and demonstrated new and better moves and equipment. Victoria and Vancouver put ice hockey on artificial ice and began the trend to extend the length of the season.

CHAPTER 5

Professionalism, Spectator Loyalties, and Team Rivalries

Professionalism

Professionalism crept or stormed into amateur hockey, depending on how you look at it. It was in the very early 1900s that the matter got sorted out, in the midst of many a heated battle, tongue lashing, name calling, and team suspension. In those early years of hockey excitement, children and adults alike, bitten by the hockey bug, began asking, "Which town has the best hockey team? Who's going to win the trophy?" And it was a matter of some importance to them.

A single outstanding player could often make the difference. Most towns had a best player, or players, and it wasn't long before the self-appointed hockey promoters were seeing to it that their town did have a special player or two who could make the difference, secure the position of best for their home team, and win the trophy. But the CAHA was keeping a close eye on payment of players, which would make them professionals playing in an amateur league. Under-the-counter deals were being made by team owners and, when suspected, were reported by other teams and investigated. A team would quickly be disqualified and suspended if league officials found that a player was being paid to play.

The legitimate way to get around the problem was to entice a good player to come to town by offering him a good job at a very good salary. This often meant paying him much more than the job was worth. Then again, if he scored goals and entertained the town, it was worth it, and it was wonderful to have such a good citizen living and working in town. By 1907, professionalism scored the goal it was headed for and became accepted, particularly in Ontario and Quebec. As the pros took over the bigger teams, including the bigger trophies (like the Stanley Cup), the smaller towns were still heavily involved in amateur hockey. League rules eventually relaxed to allow each team no more than two (and later four) professional players, imported in order to maintain the quality of hockey demanded by the fans. New trophies were offered and players and teams struggled to be champions as if their lives depended on it. And the fans ate it up.

Spectator Loyalties

As spectators developed deep-seated team loyalties, fights often broke out in the crowd over minor matters. Objects were thrown on the ice, windows and lights broken, and chairs toppled from the gallery to the ice below on rougher occasions. Train car loads of fans often arrived at the rinks for special games. There are many examples of fans fighting outside the rinks and on the way to and from the railway station when spirits were especially high. But of all the fan feuds that arose from team loyalties, the greatest ever to occur in Nova Scotia, and perhaps in all of Canada, was triggered over paid players in the Sydney-Glace Bay series of 1941.

Glace Bay vs. Sydney — A Fight Over "Miner" Matters

Any hockey team having players with names like "Tiger" Mackie, "Legs" Fraser, "Kink" MacDonald, "Jo Jo" Grabowski, and "Leaky" Boates, has got to have a good story or two to tell. The one about the rivalry between the fans in the towns of Glace Bay, where these characters played for a team called the Glace Bay Miners, and the fans of the Millionaires in nearby Sydney, Cape Breton, has got to be the classic tale of two towns pitted against each other. Glace Bay, which at that time had a population of 25,000, was a coal town, and Sydney, with 28,000, was known as the "steel city." Close neighbours, they had always been interdependent commercially, but when it came to hockey, they hated each other. In the war years, the CAHA allowed no more than four paid players on any amateur team, and that was to maintain a good quality of play. The Miners, however, had an excess of these so-called "SHAMateur" players. Ten in all, to be exact. And when the eligibility of two of them was questioned and the Miners ended up losing one of their best forwards and their goalie, they were in deep trouble heading into the playoffs, because their substitute goalie, "Leaky" Boates, wasn't capable of saving the day! Now the Miners' mentor, one Marty MacDonald, who had just lost two of his gang of "hired hands," had to play his cards close to his chest if he was going to outsmart Sydney and win the series. It was 45 years before Marty finally told his friends what he did, all for the sake of the game! A war-time rule declared that players who "joined up" could be replaced. So Marty simply offered Leaky Boates $200 to join the army! When Leaky said that he didn't want to go to war, Marty gave him $100 and a ticket to Montreal on the night train and told him to disappear for a while. Next day, Leaky was gone and nobody knew where. The plan came together and a wonderful goalie named "Legs" Fraser joined the Miners and led Glace Bay to two straight wins. But then the submerged Leaky Boates surfaced and was spotted by a reporter in Truro. It turned out that Boates didn't know anybody in Montreal and thought he'd be lonesome, so he got off the train in nearby Truro. The jig was up, and Marty phoned Boates and told him to get back to Glace Bay and to bring his $100 with him. Leaky came back and performed poorly as predicted, and Glace Bay lost the series. The victorious Sydney Millionaires went on to vie for the Allan Cup.

Family Feuds

During the height of the controversy, citizens of the two towns learned just how deep fan loyalty can become, for members of families had bitter fights: Glace Bay retailers installed a roadblock and refused to allow Sydney wholesalers in their shops, Sydney folks could not eat in Glace Bay restaurants, and there was talk of the coal miners going on strike, which would shut down the steel city operation. One family story that indicates just how far the fan feud went concerns a Sydney woman and her favourite older cousin in Glace Bay. The two would frequently be in touch on the phone in the evening (when the rates were lowest) to chat and affirm their lifelong admiration for each other. When the hockey battle was at its height, they got on the phone in the middle of the afternoon without regard for cost and had it out with each other. They then refused to speak to one another for several months thereafter, even though neither had ever attended a single hockey game or set foot in a rink in their entire lives. Now that's how loyal fans can get toward their home town teams in Nova Scotia!

THINGS WERE NO BETTER IN NEW BRUNSWICK: "WE WANT OUR MONEY BACK" — In 1905, a newspaper in New Brunswick ran an article entitled "Lively Time in Fredericton," which described the fan reaction at a play-off match between the Fredericton Trojans and the Marysville Crescents, which was to decide the championship of York County. The Marysville team had been promised a $25 guarantee, and when it was not forthcoming, they simply refused to come on the ice for the second period. When the rink manager couldn't be found, the game was called off and the fans, disappointed about not getting their money back, broke windows, tore down light fixtures, crashed seats to the ice from the balcony, turned water on the ice, and tore down decorations, requiring the police to clear the rink. The reporter closed by stating, "not even at a time of Canada's greatest achievements during the South African war were there such unruly crowds on the streets of the city and it was midnight before police got the crowd, who were clambering for their money back, to go home."

The women playing ice hockey on the Island in that era called their teams the Abbie Sisters and the Crystal Sisters.

SKATING RINK, WINDSOR, 1899 —
Following a fire in 1897 that
destroyed the town, including its
first covered rink, this rink was built
at a time when most other Canadian
towns were building their first rink.
When the management deemed
it wise to cancel skating in the
afternoon in order to ensure good
ice for an important night hockey
game, season ticket holders were
admitted to the game in lieu of their
lost skating session.

Postcard, Valentine and Sons

CHAPTER 6

Outdoor Skating in Nova Scotia

Northern Europeans, principally Scandinavians, Finns, and Dutch, were the first to use bone runners (held to their feet with thongs), mostly for hunting. The English are known to have used them in the 12th and the Dutch in the 14th century. Hand-held sticks were used for propulsion. Skates made from animal bones and walrus teeth have been discovered in England, Germany, the Netherlands, Finland, and Austria. The word "skate" means shank or leg bone. The Norse added a metal runner to skis and created the forerunner of the stock skate, which was developed in Scotland. Stock (block) skates consist of wrought-iron blades imbedded in stocks, or blocks of wood. These were attached to boots with a leather thong or rope strap system, which had to be retightened from time to time and partly cut off the circulation of the feet. Peasants, using skates to get to work or market, developed speed, whereas the nobility, using skates for sheer pleasure, are responsible for developing grace and elegance on blades. Later models of skates in the 1700s had short spikes that stuck into the soles of boots for added security, and still later a screw was used to hold the stock to the heel of the boot. This added security led to "fancy skating," the forerunner of figure skating.

Scotland, the Birthplace of Sport Skating

There had been skating on bone blades and wooden blades previously and elsewhere, but not until the iron-blade skate was devised in Scotland in 1572 did an interest in recreational skating lead to the development of the sport. Skating, as a sport, began in Scotland, where there was a skating club in Edinburgh as early as 1642. When the Scots came to Nova Scotia, they brought their skates with them.

In the late 1700s, ice skating was very popular in Nova Scotia. Most people started to skate early in life. With none of the present-

Skating Race. The Start.

SPEED SKATERS ON OUTDOOR ICE SURFACE — **Skating races, preceding hockey games, were common across the country in the early 1900s.**

Postcard, Raphael Tuck & Sons

day modes of winter entertainment available, skating took prime place on the list of things to do during the three months that natural ice was available. Skating as couples, hand in hand or arm in arm, was a favourite pastime, and for many couples it was the way they courted in winter. Often couples ended up skating through life together.

Swarms of People

On clear winter days, into the 1800s, skaters of all ages swarmed onto the ponds and lakes and gathered for exercise and the sociability of the sport. There was no scarcity of places to skate. With so many people involved, everybody had their favourite place or places to skate, and somebody was out at every opportunity, clearing the ice to ensure the smoothest surface possible, for all to enjoy. Each pond had its own name, and most people in a town were familiar with all and used each of them at some time or another, for depending on conditions, one was sometimes better than another. Small hand-held candle lanterns lit up the outdoor ice surfaces in the evening as skaters glided along in a joyous mood. Bonfires, tended by men and admired by curious young boys, added light for skating and provided heat to warm fingers, cheeks, and toes. Chairs equipped with runners allowed older folk and those weak of leg to

get into the fun as they were pushed about the ice. All the while the young ones darted in and out, back and forth, playing chase and tag. Stock skates were the common skate of the day. Many block skates were handmade by local craftsmen, and no two pair were exactly alike.

Fancy Skaters and Figure Eights

Some were better skaters than others, and the more skilled could cut letters and figures in the ice, skate backwards, and even twirl on the spot. To be able to carve your whole name in the ice was the ultimate achievement for the accomplished skater. Fancy skating was the proper term to describe these acrobatics that were developing on the ice surfaces of Nova Scotia as skatists tried to outdo one another with new figures. Fancy skating was developing in several countries at the time, and was clearly the forerunner to figure skating.

The Practical Skater

People who lived on the shores of rivers and lakes often skated to and from school and work. Country folk on the Bras d'Or Lakes in Cape

THE GRAND MARCH, AT A WINTER CARNIVAL, HALIFAX — The skaters are wearing a mixture of stock skates (with leather straps) and the new spring skates, which clamped onto boots. The Halifax Skating Rink, built in 1862, opened for skating on January 3, 1863.

PANS

ABORIGINAL COSTUMES — **Skaters at an ice carnival in Native costumes.**

PANS

Breton skated regularly to work in Baddeck. Sometimes they would meet the country doctor crossing the ice with his horse and sleigh on his way to or from a house call. People travelled between farms for visits as well as work, and often skated to church when roads were deep with snow and lakes were blown clear by winter winds. On open stretches, with a breeze from behind, a good skater could cover 20 to 30 miles an hour.

Skates for Sale

In the 1820s, with skating well established as a favourite winter pastime, the demand for skates was great, and Halifax merchants were even advertising stock skates, imported from England, in Windsor's daily paper, the Windsor *Mail*.

Indoor Covered Rinks

It wasn't until the 1860s that ice skating became popular enough to initiate the construction of covered rinks that would allow people to skate regardless of outdoor weather conditions. Since so many skaters detested ice hockey and hockeyists so badly, one has to wonder if there wasn't an ulterior motive for building rinks, in Nova Scotia at least, because ice hockey was not allowed and the skaters had the new rinks all to themselves.

GRAND SKATING CARNIVAL —
The skaters are wearing Acme Club spring skates, introduced by the Starr Manufacturing Company in 1862 and patented in 1866.

PANS

Starr Spring Skates Arrive

Ice skating got a big break in 1865 when the Acme Club spring skate appeared on the market and made skating one hundred per cent easier and more enjoyable. Skates could be applied to boots quickly and more securely with the newly devised spring apparatus. The price was right, and everybody wanted (and many people got) a new pair of self-fastening "Starr skates, famous the world over." For years thereafter, the Starr Manufacturing Company led the way in skates for both skatists and hockeyists.

Windsor Skating Rink.

COMPLIMENTARY

ADMIT ONE.

J. C. SMITH, Manager.　　　　JOHN P. SMITH, Secretary.

WINDSOR SKATING RINK, 1870-97 — One of the first covered rinks built in the country, the Windsor Skating Rink was built on Fort Edward, near the garrison, for the use of the townspeople, the military and King's College.

PANS

The Speed Skater

The 100-yard dash and the one-mile race became popular ice sports with the faster skaters. Soon competitions developed and medals and medallions were being collected by Nova Scotia's best. Many of the speed skaters became the fastest and showiest hockey players, as the game developed in the late 1800s. Certainly there were speed skating competitions before every major ice hockey match.

No Sudden Changes

As new sticks, shin pads, pucks, and rules appeared during the evolution of ice hockey in Nova Scotia, the old ones weren't necessarily discarded right away. On the contrary, many remained around for years, continuing to serve as they had served. And so it was with stock skates, for even though Starr spring skates were invented in 1865 and became world famous, homemade stock skates continued to serve many people for years to come. (Indeed, they are used in the Netherlands to this day.) The art of creating a pair of stock skates is fascinating, as you'll see when reading Ron Caplan's story of one of Cape Breton's skate-making blacksmiths, Alec Matheson.

Windsor Skating Rink,

F. A. ROACH = MANAGER

AFTERNOON SEASON TICKET

DECEMBER 25, 1924 to MARCH 25, 1925

Miss Catherine Anslow

SKATING EVERY AFTERNOON **3.30** to **5**   SATURDAY **2** to **4.30**

Covered Rinks and Indoor Skating

Although ice hockey is loved in Nova Scotia today, its current popularity was not quickly achieved. For the first 84 years that the game was played in Nova Scotia, it was played outside. Canada's first covered rinks were built by private subscription, belonged to members of the skating rinks, and were for skating only.

When the Halifax Skating Rink was built in 1862, it was the first covered rink in Nova Scotia and allowed skaters to pursue their favourite winter pastime out of the weather, every day, all winter long. No more would stormy days deny them their passion for skating. No longer would they have to shovel and scrape ponds and spots on lakes in order to don the blades. And now that they had achieved this goal, they certainly were not going to share it with those pesky hockey players! And to be certain that everybody adhered to rules, they were written in the Skating Club bylaws.

New Skates for a New Rink

John Forbes, a clerk in John Starr's Halifax hardware store, sold lots of skates and was tired of hearing skaters complain about the problems associated with stock skates. He also realized that skating remained popular in spite of the skate problems. He was likewise well aware of the new game of ice hockey developing all around him. John's father had been an inventor in Scotland, and John was

SEASON TICKET — Built in 1899, Windsor's second covered rink served the town for its second period of ice hockey.

Katherine "Kay" Anslow

inclined the same way. He was busy inventing a new skate that would put an end to the problems of skatists and hockeyists alike. His new spring skate was just ready for production the year the new covered skating rink was opened. Imagine the thrill of skating in an indoor rink with shiny new skates that easily clamped onto regular boots! No more frozen leather straps and buckles to fuss with. The poor hockeyists, of course, were still confined to the outdoors. They were not appreciated, not liked, and not allowed in the rink.

Band Concerts in the Rink

Windsor's first covered rink was built in 1870, shortly after those of Halifax and Montreal, and others followed gradually. Military and town bands played live concerts at least a couple of nights a week in most of the new rinks, and their music played a big part in the development of some of the smoothest skaters in the land. Band music was responsible for teaching the nation to skate in time and keep in step. (It was Canada's first attempt at Participaction.) Skating morning, noon, and night in those old barnlike covered rinks remained very popular for the youth of the nation through the long winter months for decades.

Winter Carnivals

Fancy dress ice carnivals were held in covered rinks yearly and formed an important part of the social life of the community. They were widely advertised, well attended, and carefully reported in the local newspapers.

Glowing accounts of prize-winning costumes were common. Children and adults, dressed as kings and scoundrels, actors and clowns, skated and competed for Best Costume prizes.

At Last, Hockey Played Inside

The city of Montreal built its magnificent Victoria Skating Rink the same year as Halifax, and the two rinks opened within days of each other. When ice hockey reached Montreal from Halifax, it was quickly embraced by the local sportsmen, and gained access to the skating rink almost immediately. The ironic thing is that it was a Halifax native, J.G.A., Creighton, who, through his influence as a figure skating judge, brought hockey into the rink. Having taught his friends in Montreal how to play the game, he joined them for practices for two seasons prior to an actual hockey match in public.

Windsor Skating Rink

BUSTIN & GLASSEY, MANAGERS.

SEASON TICKETS NOW ON SALE.

HANTS JOURNAL AD, 1920 — Season tickets for afternoon skating were $2 for the season. Most children had them.

The game, played on March 3, 1875, was the first public hockey match played inside a covered rink anywhere. It was not until February of 1884, following a winter carnival in Sarre's Rink, that Haligonians got to see their first hockey game played inside.

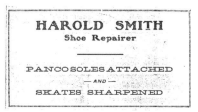

HANTS JOURNAL AD, 1923 — Shoemakers attached new skates to boots with rivets after the little screws gave way to hockey's stress. They also sharpened skates "While You Wait" on the way to the rink.

Electric Lights

In the 1890s, the new electric streetlights were installed "for early evening use only" in many Canadian towns and cities. It wasn't long before people began having electricity installed in their homes. For the most part this consisted of bare bulbs in sockets suspended from the ceiling with twisted, cloth-covered insulated wires and operated at first by an overhead pull chain, often with a long string attached and later by clever wall switches. Soon, lights were installed in rinks as well.

Skating and Hockey at Night

Electric lights ushered in a new phase of spectator sport: ice hockey in rinks at night. A slight problem arose, however, when the odd stray puck happened to connect with a light and sent it crashing to the ice below, holding up the game while the broken glass was cleared from the ice.

Lights in the Rink: Night Skating

Covered rinks and electric lights allowed Canadians to enjoy skating and ice hockey into the night regardless of wind or weather. What excitement to skate under the lights to rousing marches and melodic waltzes played by the town band.

First Victrolas, Then Electric Turntables

When hand-wound, spring-powered Victrolas were replaced with electric turntables, "canned" music took over in rinks for the most part. The common sound was of waltzes and marches played over loudspeakers from scratchy, over-used 78s. The town band still appeared at ice carnivals and other special events and remained a big hit with those smooth skaters. In that era, most of the skaters were every bit as graceful as the figure skaters who are seen on TV these days. The popularity and the art of graceful skating in a community setting seems to have declined in recent years. The common choice

EVANS & CO. SKATE AD, 1931-32.

of music used for entertainment during skating sessions in many rinks these days does not stimulate either good timing or graceful strokes of the blades.

Starrs for Skatists and Hockeyists

The Starr Manufacturing Company presented a continual line of new and better ice skates, figure skates, and hockey skates for many years. Professionals and amateurs all over the globe looked to Starr for the best and got it. For seven decades, by far the greater proportion of skaters and hockey players in Canada's covered rinks used nothing but the best: Starr skates.

Skatists and Hockeyists, Together at Last

By the 1890s, ice hockey had finally gained favour with folks across the nation, and it suddenly seemed all right for it to be played indoors. Skatists and hockeyists were beginning to share ice time in Canada's first covered rinks. Plans were made to build covered rinks as joint projects for the benefit of skaters and hockey players alike. What a magnificent idea! What a great Canadian community plan! By 1900, covered rinks were popping up almost everywhere and becoming the centre of social life of most communities for the entire winter season.

As artificial ice technology became generally affordable in the 1930s and 1940s, ice plants were installed in some of the old rinks, but mostly communities saw the chance to build new and better rinks with modern ice-making facilities that would serve another generation or two. The old rinks were either used for some other purpose or simply allowed to age and decay.

Gone but Not Forgotten

The arrival of movies, television, and other ways of spending leisure winter time has doubtless altered the skating habits of Canadians. True, people still skate, and they still skate together, and hockey is played more than ever. But it's not the same somehow. The construction of covered rinks set the stage for something new and different to occur in Canada. Skating and ice hockey had moved indoors on new skates. Neither would ever be the same again. Those of us who were privileged to be a part of the excitement of that era had an experience that is difficult to describe. It was something unique which made our lives different from those who went before us, and something which few who follow us will ever know about.

Covered Rink vs. Sportsplex

The covered rinks did much to bring Canadian people together as a social unit, and doubtless the now common community sportsplex is serving the same purpose in a slightly different way. But stepping into a sportsplex anywhere across the nation these days just doesn't give one the same sensation, or thrill, that swept over us when we crowded into those spruce-shingled, weathered, wooden rinks to do some fancy skating or to watch or take part in amateur ice hockey, small town style!

Just as fancy skating on ponds (using stock skates) developed into figure skating and hurley-on-ice developed into ice hockey, so the old covered rinks of our nation have been redesigned as the sportsplex. Stock skates, Starr skates and hurley sticks can be found in Hockey Heritage Centres in Windsor, Dartmouth, and Halifax, but few of Canada's old covered rinks remain to give one a sense of what life was like when our winter sports came in out of the cold.

Making Ice: Natural vs. Artificial

Beginning in 1911, hockey players in Vancouver and Victoria were the first in Canada to play on the new surface. That year, Lester and Frank Patrick, members of hockey's famous Patrick family of Nelson, B.C., organized the Pacific Coast Hockey Association. They also built the Victoria Arena and Vancouver's Denham Arena, both equipped with artificial ice. Their creativity established professional hockey in the West and ushered in a most significant phase in the ongoing evolution of Canada's great game. Ice hockey, which had started as a strictly amateur recreational activity back in Nova Scotia, had become an organized professional game all across the nation. The activity which had struggled to be accepted in its early stages, in the province of its origin, was now obviously embraced and loved in the entire country. Although it wasn't yet labelled as such, everybody understood that ice hockey had actually become Canada's national winter sport.

Before long, artificial ice was introduced into arenas in other cities, but not until the 1950s was it common in small-town rinks. In the meantime, all those havens of skating and ice hockey across the

ADVERTISEMENT FROM THE *ACADIAN RECORDER*, 1904.

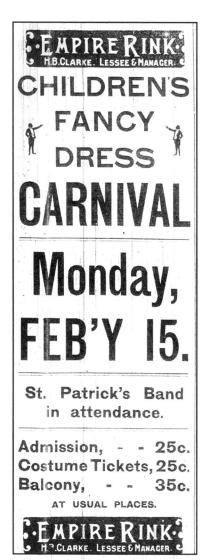

ADVERTISEMENT FROM THE *ACADIAN RECORDER,* 1904.

country had only natural ice, which was subject to the whims of Mother Nature. As Foster Hewitt said when considering winter sports in that era, hockey was a "child of the weather." In most of these towns with natural ice rinks, the game began in January and was all over by mid-March, play-offs and all.

To be sure that the best possible ice was available for the entire winter season, short as it was, one depended on having good ice makers, like those in Windsor, Nova Scotia. For years, Harry Sweet kept skatists and hockeyists content with his ice-making abilities. When Harry was too old to carry on, the Carmichael brothers, Ned and Fred, took over. These men had to watch for changes in temperature and would make ice, night and day, during cold snaps. They took shifts around the clock in order to build up as thick a layer as possible. When it was really cold, water could be sprayed on liberally with a garden hose. Otherwise it was applied in a thin film with an apparatus made from an oil barrel on wheels, with a fine spray attachment on the front. It was pushed around the ice on foot on the same route that the Zamboni takes today and did the same job, but more slowly, and on a much smaller scale. When the temperature rose, even slightly, the windows were quickly closed and boarded up to keep the rink as cold as possible and preserve the ice.

Sparks Begin to Fly

As spring approached, the sun got stronger and the season slowly came to an end. The ice got softer and thinner by the day, and eventually the sand and gravel base began to wear through here and there and skates started catching on the undersurface. While sparks flew from hockey players' skates, oaths usually flew from their lips. Bodies began tripping and sprawling over the ice at most inopportune times.

The Cry Goes Out: "Snow the Ice"

The other problem that confronted players toward the end of the season was the ever-present puddles that occurred as temperatures hovered around the freezing mark. Trying in desperation to maintain a dry surface for an all-important game, Ned and Fred would have to get the rink rats to snow the ice, to sop up the water, and scrape it just before the players were ready to begin. Spot checks would have to take place between periods as well. Soft ice slowed the game, and weather was the ruler of the rinks.

Recycling Newspapers

On occasion, between periods, newspapers would be placed on thin puddles to pick up water. Often a sheet would refuse to come away from the ice again, allowing the players to read the headlines while looking down for the face-off.

Watching a Falling Star

One of the Toronto Maple Leafs' stars, who left the NHL to fight for his country, was playing for the Deep Brook, N.S., Navy Team in the 1940s and made the trip to Windsor on a DAR Hockey Special train, to play a game with the #1 Army Transit Camp Team of Windsor. Interviewed by Bob Mills of the local *Hants Journal* before the game over the loudspeaker system of the old Stannus Street Rink, gentleman Bob Goldham greeted the Windsor fans with a nice message and said he hoped they would enjoy seeing NHL-style hockey played through the evening. It was one of those soft nights toward the season's end, and poor Bob wasn't able to deal with ice conditions any better than the locals, NHL experience notwithstanding. It wasn't long before he hit one of those darned bare spots and slid for 10 feet, face down. For a moment there was an embarrassing silence, broken by the loud voice of a slightly inebriated fan who shouted, "Now he's showing us how they do the breast stroke in the NHL!"

Artificial Is Best

Later that evening, one of the town officials was apologizing to Bob for not having artificial ice in the rink when Bob replied, "Golly, sir, that's the most artificial ice I've ever seen!"

Praise the Ice Makers

Ice makers had to be skilled and dedicated, part manual labourer, part weatherman. Their job was like babysitting — they had to be alert to possible changes at all times. Natural ice required the ice makers to build up four or more inches of ice and struggle to protect it throughout the ten weeks of cold weather. Knowing this, one realizes the importance of artificial ice to the progress of the development of the game over the years. One quarter of an inch of artificial ice is all that's needed for skating or ice hockey.

An artificial ice skating rink had been built in Southport, near Liverpool, in England as early as 1882, but it was years later before it was introduced to Canada. Ice hockey was first played on our East Coast; artificial ice was first used on the West Coast.

STOCK BLOCK SKATES — Ron Caplan chose Cape Breton Island, Nova Scotia, as his home more than 20 years ago, and he spends his time creating word-and-picture portraits of elements of Cape Breton life for *Cape Breton's Magazine*, which he edits and has published all those years. He has kindly granted permission to reprint on the following pages his description and pictures of Alex Matheson creating a pair of stock (block) skates.

Ron Caplan

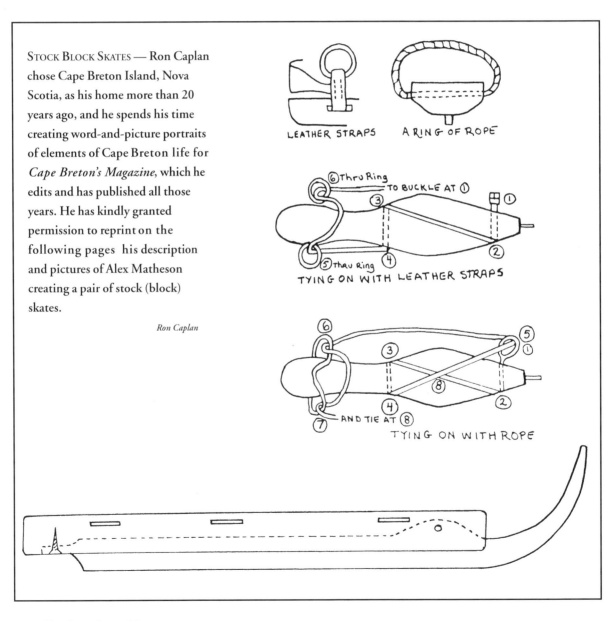

A Pair of Stock Skates

by Ron Caplan

Stock skates were the first kind of ice skates used on Cape Breton. Some people call them block skates. They were followed by the spring skates which clipped onto the shoe, fiercely gripping the heel and often ripping it off. And these were followed by the full shoe and hockey skates we know today. But it was the stock skates people used here years ago when the winters seemed frostier and the scholars around the island could be seen skating to and from school. Alex Matheson took his skates to school, and dried them by the stove. He was born in 1898, at a place called Big Hill. He's been a blacksmith since 1919, and one of the few whose forge (at South Haven) still sees fire.

Recently, he made a pair of stock skates from a bar of quarter-inch by one-inch Swedish steel (children's skates long ago were often made from an old rasp), a quarter-inch rod of iron, some wire, two screws and two blocks of ash. He used no mould or pattern beyond a simple tracing to be certain the blocks would be both longer and considerably narrower than the feet of the man who would use them. He worked with only the memory of a finished pair of skates, and a knowledge of what happens to certain metals when they are heated and struck.

To start a fire, he made a little space in the spent coal at the opening of the forge and put in a handful of shavings. He lit the

shavings and turned the blast on gently. The air comes up from below and is sucked up the chimney. He built the coal up at the sides to create a good draft, and let the green coal — the soft coal — burn till he had red coals. Some of the days he worked were bitter cold and oddly there was no heat from the forge. When it is right, the chimney sucks up all the gas and smoke, and most of the heat.

He took the bar of steel and put an end in the fire and left it there. The fire was kept small, just enough to heat up the section to be worked. He took the bar out bright red on the end and put it on top of the anvil and with the ball peen hammer, he beat the very end to one-half inch

"The most of the tools are made right here. All the chisels are made, the punches. You'd buy an anvil and a blower, a vice and dies, press drill . . . but all the tongs, I made them all here. Everybody did . . . . You get a bar of tool steel — you buy that — and make whatever kind of tool you want." Alex Matheson.

wide and one-eighth inch thick. This would be the heel of one blade. He put the end to the fire again, set it on the anvil and punched a hole for the screw. It was a job really requiring three hands. Alex did it with one hand holding the hammer, one hand holding the punch, the punch itself pressing the hot steel to the anvil while Alex neatly balanced the rest of the bar across his knee. Once through the metal, he put the end over the hardy hole and worked the punch to the desired size hole.

He next beat the top edge (the edge that will fit up into the wood) to a thin, feather edge. It is not simply a matter of heating and beating. The flattening and drawing out of both sides of the top edge tends to bring the bottom edge arcing around — and the bottom must be flat. So, beginning at the heel, he heated the metal and beat his way toward

Above: Pounding flat the red hot end of a bar of steel, making the blade.
Above middle: Punching a screw hole to fix the blade to the block.
Above right: Shaping along the length of the blade.
Middle Right: Little River resident John Angus MacQueen holds the blade with tongs while Alex Matheson punches a hole in the humped portion of the blade. This is where the front of the blade is fixed to the block.
Left: The upturned front of the blade is shaped.
Middle Left: Sharpening the blade at the grindstone.

Above (left to right): Shaping the block from ash; chiselling out slots for the straps; chiselling out the slot to receive the blade.

Below: Making the iron rings to go with leather straps. (Clockwise from upper-left)

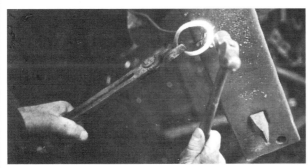

the toe, working on a few inches each heating. He beat on one side, then the other — and the top edge thinned and the whole bar bent. He put the bar on edge and straightened it out. Then he heated the bar, thinned some more on each side, and straightened it out again. The feathered portion runs straight until just before the upturn at the toe. Here he draws the metal out beyond the feathered edge, to a sort of hump that will go up further into the wood. This hump he heated and punched through. In the photograph, John Angus MacQueen, a blacksmith from Little River, is holding the blade in tongs with the hump just over an ordinary nut. When Alex Matheson punched, the punch went into the nut, making a clean

hole. Then Alex heated the blade once more and rounded the front into a half circle over the horn of the anvil.

The blades were sharpened on a grindstone, first squaring the bottom and then grinding the slightest concave groove running down the center of the length of the blade.

Alex made the blocks from ash. He roughed out the shape with an axe and then whittled the form he wanted. The blocks of stock skates are like a boat, the blades the keel. The blocks are much narrower than the foot that rides them, and continue to taper to the blade. They are made so that there is the least chance of wood touching the ice. The openings for the straps are 1-by-1/4 inch slots, cut 5/16 inch down from the top of the block. He first drilled three holes in from

each side with a 3/4 inch drill, then chiselled out the slot. He worked from both sides toward the centre, and once open he ran a hot bar of metal through the slot. He finished the three slots, then turned the block bottom up in the vice, drew a line down the centre, sawed on the line to get started — then chiselled out a slot to receive the feathered edge of the blade. He chipped a space wide enough at the heel to set the screw hole flush with the wood.

There are a number of ways of attaching the blade to the block. The block could have been drilled through from side to side and a pin driven through the hump on the blade, but Alex felt a tighter job could be had by drilling two tiny holes down from the top, putting a strong wire through the hole in the hump and feeding the ends up through the tiny holes. He gripped the wires in pliers, pulling up and twisting them together, drawing the blade tight. He drove the wires into the wood. Then he put the screw at the heel.

He made the rings of iron, a coarser material than the steel blades. He cut 7 inches of metal rod with a bolt cutter. Seven inches will give a 2-inch ring. He rounded the hot bar over the horn of the anvil, then he prepared the hot ends. The method is called "scarfing," and it is used to make ends fit without extra thickness at the joining. He heated it once more again and put a little Borax or welding compound (flux) at the scarfing and put it back in the fire. He said, "Welding is like bread. Burn it and it's no good. Leave it raw and it won't stick. You have to get accurate heat at both ends. You have to watch your metal, You know it's ready when it's *just* starting to melt." He put it on the anvil, worked the ends together, started with light taps, then heavier ones, welding the ring.

Usually the blacksmith made only the metal parts and it was left to the customer to make his own blocks, and either straps or spliced rings of rope for tying the skates on. Straps usually involved bringing an old pair of reins back to life with neat's-foot oil — then sewing on a buckle and the rings.

CHAPTER 7

Hockey Outfits and Equipment

John Cunard, who had his front teeth knocked out on Long Pond in Windsor in 1816, would attest to the fact that roughness in hockey has been there since the game began. Yet, for the first nine decades that the game was played, the players did not use any protective equipment to prevent bodily harm. All through the formative years, and even for 15 years after the game spread to Quebec and Ontario from Nova Scotia, the goalie didn't even wear pads.

The earliest visual evidence that I have found of a goalie wearing shin pads appears in a photo taken in 1889. That year, John E. Brown, the goalie for the Dartmouth Chebuctos who travelled to Montreal and Quebec for an interprovincial tournament, wore leather riding spats as shin pads. Shortly after, hockey goaltenders everywhere must have decided that their counterparts in the field game of cricket really didn't need their pads during the winter months, so they confiscated them. Cricket pads showed up in hockey team photos for the next several years. At the same time, the rest of the team appeared at matches with short, reinforced pads strapped to their shins outside of their stockings. It had only taken nine decades to solve the longstanding sore shin problem. (Technology didn't advance nearly as fast in that era as in the present one.)

Turtlenecks and Knickers

In the 1880s, quilted, over-the-knee trousers and home-knit turtleneck sweaters worn with matching knee socks were the dress of the day. The trousers had been adopted from football, of course, since many of the hockey players were also football players. Hockey teams were essentially the country's football clubs in search of an activity to keep them in shape over the winter months while waiting to get back on the football field in spring. Why wouldn't they be wearing

WINDSOR ACADEMY GIRLS HOCKEY TEAM, 1946 — These smiling sports, some wearing the older quilted trousers, some with implanted wood rods beneath the canvas for more protection from rough play, were happy showing off their trophy in their year-end photo. The goalie's mitts were still a matched pair. Thin shin guards were worn beneath stockings, and there was no other protective equipment available for these girls, who were excellent skaters and loved playing hockey, half a century ago. Front row: Celeste Quillen, Irma Vaughan, Joan Vaughan, Barbara Creed, June Bearne; back row: Betty Haley, Ardith Carson, Rhoda Palfrey, Ellen Meagher, Barbara MacDonald, Anna Baird, Carol Lohnes.

Joan Vaughan

their quilted pants? And they continued to wear them until some smart soul decided to devise a protection for kneecaps as had been done for shins.

Short Pants and Long Stockings

In the time period between 1900 and 1910, some hockey players had begun to wear full-length stockings and shorter trousers than previously for easier manoeuvrability. The short pants, called hockey knickers, with quilted padding, sold for $1 a pair, while the cheaper unpadded type cost 50 cents a pair.

Gauntlets and Gloves

The earliest version of hockey gloves, used by all players these days, did not appear until 1904. Called gauntlets at first, they were available from the Eaton's catalogue for $1.75 a pair. Photos of hockey teams prior to that time showed the players either bare-handed or wearing simple unpadded kid leather gloves, exactly the same as anybody would wear on the street. They were completely unsuited for hockey as it's played these days. Even though hockey gloves were available, many did not use them for years.

Shinpads

Year-end photos from 1896, show players with small shinpads worn outside their stockings. For some unknown reason they were short and covered the leg only from skate boot to mid-shin. Over the next few years, players began to place shinpads beneath their stockings, and, by 1912, shinpads were commonly being worn under stockings instead of outside, and were being held in place with circular strips of red rubber cut from cast-off automobile inner tubes. These garters were popular for years and were often worn outside of stockings as well. They are the predecessor of the white hockey tape commonly used for the same purpose these days. Many hockeyists made their own shinpads, well into the 1930s, by stitching thin leather over strips of hardwood (often bamboo) to a layer of dark blue harness felt which was freely available as scraps from any number of horse harness shops. Remember, it was the Depression, and people were making do with what was available at the lowest cost.

RESOLUTE HOCKEY TEAM, 1900 — Back row: Dimock, Dill, Dimock; front row: Burgess, Dimock (goalie), Burgess, Redmond. The goalie is using the same stick and shin pads as the other players. Their short shin guards cover only the lower part of the legs and give no protection to the knees. The special singles skates worn by the goalkeeper have puck stops on the blades. Most played in bare hands or work gloves, because hockey gloves (called gauntlets) were not available until 1904.

WHHC

Kneepads

A poster used by the famous Starr Manufacturing Company in Nova Scotia gives us one of our earliest ideas of the protective device used on knees. The Starr hockey player, depicted on a frozen lake, is still wearing his padded football trousers, but his knees are covered with beautifully constructed leather pads held in place with thin leather straps and buckles over the trousers. His shinpads are worn beneath his stockings and seem less bulky than their predecessors.

Around 1912, stretchy, elasticized knee covers with vertically sewn strips of white felt were being worn to protect knees and were accompanied by padded short pants and the long circular striped hockey stockings we're used to seeing today.

Cricket Pads

Goalies wearing cricket pads continued to appear in year-end championship team photos across the country until 1912, when goal pads specially designed for ice hockey appeared. The Eaton's catalogue offered them for sale at $3.50 a pair and "especially adapted for senior league hockey" at $4.50. The same year, pucks sold for 20 cents, full length hockey socks for 75 cents, and hockey knickers for $1, while goalie skates with a puck stop included on the blade cost $2 a pair (boots not included). One had to look in the local shoe store or in the boot and shoe section of the catalogue for hockey boots. They cost another $2–$4 a pair.

Elbow Pads

Elbow pads, similar to the first kneepads, came along in the early 1920s, just as goalies began protecting themselves more by wearing cricketer's or baseball catcher's chest pads. Shoulder and body pads followed shortly after and completed the basic prototype of today's hockey outfit and equipment.

Toques and Tassels

Headdress for hockey players well into the 1920s was a knitted toque, often with a tassel or ball of coloured yarn on top, as shown in the Starr skate ads and early photos. Then, for many years, players went bareheaded. The protective helmet, so well known today, made its debut in the 1930s. It first consisted of slabs of harness felt faced with leather, or a hard substance called bakelite, arranged in a

Wolfville Hockey Team: Year-End Photo, 1902-03 — Gauntlets (hockey gloves) were not yet available. The goalie still used an ordinary hockey. Leather-covered, cane shinpads, worn outside and attached with leather straps, left knees unprotected. The new single blade skates were attached with tiny screws to new hockey boots. Pants were knickers and hats were tassled toques. A central hair part was the style of the day for these young lovers of ice hockey, who looked to the future for pads for knees, elbows, shoulders, and bodies. Left to right: W. Geldert, rover; H. DeWitt, spare; W. Harris, point; A. DeWitt, centre; P. Benjamin, left wing; R. Dennier, right wing; E. Hosterman, cover point; L.S. Boates, business manager; P. Pineo, goal.

Alvin Ells

ELGRAVES HOCKEY TEAM, 1905 —
The Derby (pea-bouncer) hat
worn by Harold Anslow, editor
of the *Hants Journal,* signified
his managerial position with
the winners of the Town League
Trophy. Quilted knickers gave
the only protection yet available
for kneecaps, and these boys, in
bare hands, were still without
hockey gauntlets. Their team
name, emblazoned across their
chests, was innovative and signified
team pride.

Peter "Pete" MacKinnon

halo around the head and held in place with an elasticized chin strap.
Such helmets were used by very few players at first. As with hockey
gloves, many years passed before headgear became generally
accepted.

Soft Shoulders

Hockey was well into the 1930s before serious attention was given
to protecting the shoulders. When shoulder pads did appear, they
were disliked by many players, who continued to play without them
for several years.

Hockey Pucks

In Nova Scotia, where ice hockey evolved, "a puck in the mouth"
means a strike or hit in the face with a closed fist, as an expression
of extreme anger.

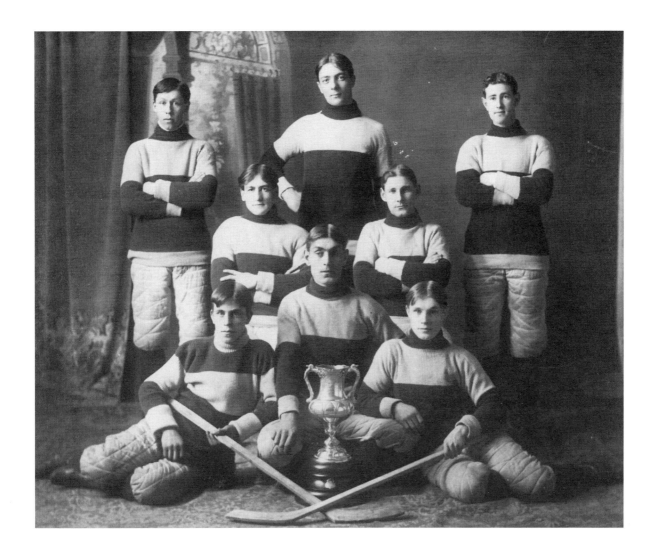

In Ireland, a "puck bird" is a robin-sized bird also called a goat sucker, which is known for diving and striking goats in fields.

To hit or slap the ball in the game of hurley (also called hurling) is to "puck it."

"Puck" Means "Strike"

In general, it appears that a "hit" or "strike" is the accepted meaning of the word puck as it applies to hurley and its Canadian offspring, ice hockey. And since, for the entire 60 minutes of every hour that the game of ice hockey is played, that's exactly what happens to the 3" x 1" elusive object that is chased about the ice, there's little wonder that it is simply called a puck.

In the ancient Irish field game of hurley, from which Canada's ice hockey evolved, the word "puck" is used both as a noun and a verb. A goaltender, when scored on, is awarded a free puck out from the

THE ELGRAVES OF WINDSOR, 1906 — The attire of the day was a turtleneck sweater and padded knickers when these young hockey stars won the Citizens' Trophy in 1906. Central hairparts seemed more important than protective equipment. Front: J. Smith, spare; F. Brown, centre; G.V. Smith, captain; middle: F. Fletcher, right wing; L.A. Shaw, rover; back: H.S. Anslow, left wing; C. Curry, cover point; J. Redmond, point.

WHHC

hand to his teammates. When a foul is called against a team, the referee awards a free puck to the opposition from the sideline, known as a sideline puck or a side puck. If the ball is hit a long distance, it is referred to as a long puck, while young hurley players learning the moves of the game are said to be pucking around.

Newfie Pucks on the Pond

In Newfoundland, where people, things, places, and events often have names peculiar to the island, the game of ice hockey has long been referred to as "pucks." Since any and all scraps of water, including the island's many lakes, are referred to as ponds, the common invitation of hockey players in the outports over the years since hockey made its way to "The Rock" has been, "Let's go play pucks on the pond, b'y!" And when they played, they often used wooden pucks in the outports, even as recently as the 1960s.

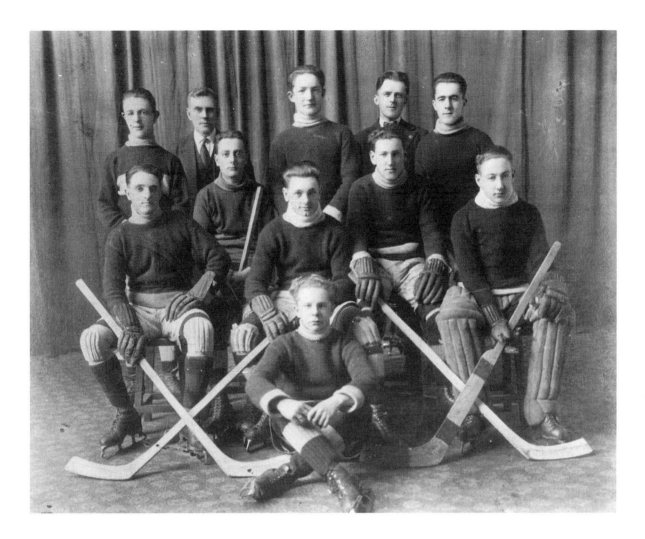

WINSOW ACADEMY SCOUTS, 1922 — Nova Scotia Junior Champions.
These young players were happy with their new elasticized, felt-ribbed
knee protectors, short pants, padded gauntlets and singles skates. Tube
skates were designed for hockey in 1900, but most players had gotten used
to singles and preferred them. It took many years to convert some to tubes.
The wide-on-one-side goalkeeper's stick remained a favourite with goalies
into the 1930s, even though a wider stick had been available since 1915.
Back row: William Chambers, William Smith (coach), Jim Bacon, Charlie
Wigmore (manager), R. MacRae. Front row: Lloyd Taylor, George
Hughes, Norman MacDonald, Cliff Shaw, John Doran. The young player
out front (with over-size skate boots) is "Doggie" Kuhn, who went on to
play for the New York Americans in the NHL a decade later.

Frances Bacon

Hurley Ball

Around 1800, when the boys at King's College School began adapting the field game of hurley to the ice of Long Pond, it would have been natural for them to use the conventional hurley ball. But, since it is almost impossible to control a bouncing ball on ice, it was equally as natural to replace it with a flat wooden puck. When hockey was in the developing stages on the ponds, lakes, and inlets of Nova Scotia in the mid-1800s, wooden pucks, cut from stovewood sticks in the back yard or from a tree limb, were in common use.

Cherry Wood Pucks Best

The Mi'kmaq, who played hurley with the garrison troops and other Nova Scotians in the 1800s, also used wooden pucks. The Mi'kmaq preferred cherry wood because the bark clung to the wood like leather and was dark coloured and easy to see against the white snow and ice.

THE PHINNEY MUSIC COMPANY LIMITED, BARRINGTON STREET, HALIFAX — A Nova Scotia enigma, a music store that sold sporting goods, is easily explained. Mr. Phinney simply loved sports as much as music!

Halifax Herald

78TH HIGHLANDERS, 1915 —
Champions of Pictou County played
on Pictou Harbour ice. They are
using Mic-Mac and Red Dot hockey
sticks. Most are wearing the popular
Starr Regal single-blade skates. The
officer and one player are wearing the
new tube skates. One player is using
gloves, but most played in bare hands,
as was the custom, even though
gauntlets were available at $4 a pair
since 1904. Cricket pads were used by
goalies for several years before goalie
pads were developed and accepted.
This team still had no goal stick,
kneepads, or elbowpads. Three
had shortened their "White-Duck
Knickers," the new style at that time.

Clyde MacDonald

Wooden Pucks in Montreal

When J.G.A. Creighton moved to Montreal from Halifax in 1872
and introduced his new friends to hockey, they played their games
with wooden discs and continued to do so for some time before rubber was introduced to the game. (The newspaper account of the first
public game in Montreal described a wooden disc being used.)

First Rubber Pucks

HE SHOOTS! HE SCORES! And it had better be a regulation,
3" x 1", solid, vulcanized, one-piece rubber disc when it crosses the
goal line these days, or there'll be no goal allowed! But it wasn't always that way with pucks and goal scoring in Canada's great winter
game of ice hockey.

The first rubber pucks were not all solid, one-piece affairs, but
rather were made of layers of rubber, cemented or laminated together. One such puck, on display in the Windsor Hockey Heritage Centre, consists of nine layers of rubber, still intact,
although it is known to be more than 85 years old. Conventional
rubber pucks weigh six ounces or 175 grams, whereas Blaine Sexton's laminated puck, which is regulation size, weighs 202 grams.

Many of the early rubber pucks had a habit of splitting in two at most crucial times — for instance, when they hit the goal post. And when one half went in the net and the other half flew off to a corner or into the crowd, a real dilemma resulted for the referee. In one such incident, the player and his team-mates yelled "GOAL!" And the other team, of course, yelled "NO GOAL!" Then a very wise fan screamed out, "Give him half a goal!" The very official referee said the object in the net was not regulation size and would not allow the score to count.

In the 1902 Stanley Cup series, when Chummy Hill of the Toronto Wellingtons split a puck on the goalpost and popped half a puck in the net against the Winnipeg Victorias, that referee was more lenient and allowed the goal to be counted.

St. George's, Toronto, OHA Junior Champions, 1899 — This team added a piece to the bottom of a blade to make a wider stick for the goalkeeper. He also got to use cricket pads. Rules still prohibited him from falling to the ice to make a save. Tube skates, hockey gloves, and protective equipment were not available.

Canadian Hockey Year Book (1923)

Fancy Pucks

All pucks were not flat surfaced in the early days of vulcanized rubber pucks. Some of the oldest team photos show pucks with an elevated circular ridge all round the edge.

THE STARR HOCKEY PLAYER — Used on Starr Manufacturing Company posters to advertise skates and Mic-Mac sticks, this player was popular as an eye-catcher. He appeared in ads for sporting goods stores, on arena bulletins, and programs all across the country.

Children's Pucks

Over the years that ice hockey was developing, young children learning to play the game used any and all ice surfaces available. Likewise, they used most anything available as a puck. In the early 1920s, child-size black rubber pucks measuring $2\frac{1}{2}$" x $\frac{3}{4}$" became available at 10 cents each. Children not fortunate enough to own one of those (and there were plenty who were that poor) would use the heel of an old boot, the bung from a molasses barrel, or a rock. Many mothers stuffed hot baked potatoes into their children's skate boots before the kids headed off to the pond to ensure that toes would be warm at the beginning of the game, if not at the end. The discarded potatoes quickly froze and could be used as goalposts today and as pucks tomorrow.

Pucks in Cape Breton

Boys who grew up learning the fine art of stickhandling on the Bras d'Or Lakes and ponds of Cape Breton Island are quick to tell you that they scored many a goal with a lump of coal.

Nova Scotia Horse Apples

From 1800 until well into the 1940s, there were lots of horse-drawn wagons in Nova Scotia's cities, towns, and villages alike. This meant that there were plenty of frozen, well-formed horse droppings on streets everywhere. Since street hockey was even more popular with young boys then than it is nowadays, the frozen horsebuns, horse apples, or horse puckies, whichever you choose to call them, were put to use on a daily basis as a substitute for pucks. The only problem with horse puckies was one of durability. A couple of good slapshots frequently resulted in fragmentation, which caused the puck to fly off in many directions into nearby snowbanks. This phenomenon, of course, was often the object of the young players' efforts!

THE KANANITES AND THE ROLLED-EDGE PUCK, 1913 — The puck on display in this photo shows a very definite raised, rolled edge. Note the shinpads worn by this Nova Scotian goalkeeper. She is holding the new, wider goalie stick, handmade by the Mi'kmaq carvers of the province. A short time later, ladies' teams began using serge bloomers instead of ice-length skirts, so as to display their newly acquired leather-covered cane shinpads and to allow for a speedier game. The "avant garde" lady hockeyists were keeping up with the current hockey trends! How about those hats?

NSSHC

REGULATION WOODEN PUCK —
Vulcanized rubber was invented
by Charles Goodyear in 1839,
but it was not used for puck
construction until the 1880s. In
1886, an official ruling was adopted
by the Amateur Hockey Association
of Canada designating the 3" x 1"
vulcanized rubber disc as the
"official" puck of the association.
Up until that time, wooden
pucks were used as the game of ice
hockey developed in Nova Scotia
and Quebec.

Garth Vaughan

THE "BLAINE SEXTON" MULTI-LAYERED
PUCK — Not all rubber pucks were
one-piece regulation vulcanized
units. This puck, found in the attic
of international hockey star Blaine
Sexton, was used before World War I
and is seen to have nine layers. The
Sexton antique puck weighs
27 grams more than a conventional
rubber puck these days. The letters
"B" on one side and "S" on the
other identify the famous owner.
The presence of cuts, gouges, and
scars reflect the excessive use of this
ice hockey treasure.

Garth Vaughan

Mi'kmaq Hockeys — The Best

Nova Scotia's Mi'kmaq craftsmen were Canada's first hockey stick
makers and carried on their craft for nearly a century. Well into the
1930s, thousands of their handmade sticks were shipped yearly to
hockey enthusiasts all across Canada and the United States. Having
made sticks for hockey in Nova Scotia in the formative years of the
game, the Native carvers developed their craft into a major home
industry once the demand for sticks came from Boston, Quebec,
and Ontario. Their children joined them in harvesting the raw ma-

NOT ALL PUCKS WERE THE SAME —
A collection of wooden pucks cut
from store wood.

Garth Vaughan

WINDSOR'S NEW TROPHIES AND ODD PUCK — The Citizens' Trophy (right), won three years in a row, became a "keeper." A new and more elaborate cup took its place, and teams competed for it annually over the decades. The puck, unlike today's model, had a raised, rolled edge like others of that era. In 1897, the team had won a medallion, which was the customary prize before the cup became a popular form of recognition and praise.

Garwin Smith

terial from the forest, and the Mi'kmaq supported themselves with the industry into the 1930s, when the machine age ushered in laminated hockey sticks.

Ironwood for a Tough Job

Hornbeam, a variety of tree that provided a wood with great strength and durability, was the choice of the Mi'kmaq when they began carving Canada's first hockey sticks in Nova Scotia. Because of its characteristics, hornbeam is also called ironwood. Somewhat similar to the more common birch tree, generally known to Canadians, hornbeam once grew in great stands in its native Nova Scotia. A good woodsman will spot a hornbeam tree while walking through the woods, but generally speaking, they are difficult to find since they have been in short supply in the province for many years.

When trees were first harvested in Canada's oldest province a couple of centuries ago, they were referred to as first-growth trees. The crop of young sturdy trees that replaced them, of course, was called second-growth. It was those second growth hornbeam trees that the Mi'kmaq chose to become the nation's first hockey sticks.

"K" STANDS FOR KING'S COLLEGE, KNEEPADS, AND KNICKERS — Around 1912, when kneepads were developed, they were worn outside of stockings. The quilted knickers, which had been worn over the knees to provide some degree of protection prior to that time, were then cut to make quilted short pants, the forerunner of today's hockey pants. Here, young Blaine Sexton of Windsor (then a student at King's College in Windsor and who later became Britain's outstanding hockey star) was playing for the college team using his Starr Regal single-blade hockey skates, the choice of hockeyists all across Canada. To go with Regal skates, the Starr Company supplied the popular Rex one-piece hockey stick.

Carrie McCann

Ontario Hockeyists Loved Mi'kmaq Sticks

As hockey became popular in Ontario, the demand for choice Nova Scotia sticks was so great that the supply of hornbeam simply gave out. The Mi'kmaq picked yellow birch as their second choice for strong, durable sticks.

Starr Manufacturing to the Rescue

Around the turn of the century, when hockey was finally entrenched from coast to coast and being played by thousands in all provinces, so many sticks were required that it became impossible for the Mi'kmaq carvers to keep up with the demand. The Starr Manufacturing Company, which had been supplying skates in great numbers to satisfied hockeyists, began making hockey sticks as well. They used second-growth yellow birch and patented the Mic-Mac stick, in honour of the Native carvers. Soon after, they introduced the Rex brand stick as a partner for their popular Regal hockey skate. Ads for these Starr sticks read, "The grain of the wood runs with the curve of the blade, and they are thereby far superior to the old fashioned steam-bent sticks."

Steam-Bent Sticks

Shortly after ice hockey became popular in Ontario in the late 1880s, factories which had been making handles for farm implements began making hockey sticks by the steam-bending method. Large blocks of rock elm or ash were steamed, then bent by mechanical pressure, and kiln-dried in their altered shape. The bending device was then removed and the block, which held its new hockey shape, was sliced into several single hockey sticks. They were relatively easy and fast to produce in mass numbers. These steam-bent sticks often proved unsatisfactory because on becoming wet, which they were bound to do (especially toward spring when the ice was damp), they straightened out to a degree. Likewise, if they were left outside over a rainy spring night, they quickly lost their shape.

The Nova Scotia sticks held their natural curved shape and remained popular for decades.

Mic-Mac Still Best

The fall and winter edition of the Eaton's catalogue in 1904 offered Mic-Mac brand, handmade, yellow birch, oil-finished hockey sticks for 39 cents each. A team lot of a dozen cost $4.50. The 1913-14 Eaton's catalogue noted that they were still the choice of the Ontario Hockey Association.

FEATURED IN 1915 — This 1915 photo shows singles goalie skates with puck stops, Mic-Mac sticks, and the new tube skates with ankle supports.

Clyde MacDonald

FREE PUCK AD FROM THE *HANTS JOURNAL*, JANUARY 12, 1938.

MIC-MAC HOCKEY STICK — From the 1905 Starr skate book.

REX HOCKEY STICK — From the 1905 Starr skate book.

The Starr Guarantee

The label on a Starr stick, recently retrieved from Kitchener, Ontario, is on display in the Windsor Hockey Heritage Centre and states that Starr sticks were crafted to "meet the requirements of the best players." They were available in left-hand or right-hand models. The handles had longitudinal grooves "ensuring firm grip and preventing slipping." The sticks were "specially made for forwards, defence and goal," and so durable that many players, particularly goal tenders, used their favourites for several seasons.

The Rex stick had a popular feature in the "double-grooved blade, the lower one being serrated, enabling accurate shooting of puck for goal, and strengthening the hockey stick." Starr ads asserted that their designs were "fully covered at Ottawa" and warned that "infringers would be prosecuted."

Mic-Mac and Rex brand sticks were made and distributed by the Starr Manufacturing Company of Dartmouth in their many outlets as well as other sport stores and hardware stores across the nation and in the U.S. They could be obtained by mail from Eaton's, Simpson's, and the Hudson's Bay Company, along with the world-famous Starr skates.

Recently, one of the early versions of the Mic-Mac stick, shipped from Nova Scotia, turned up in Peterborough, Ontario. The antique is only 44 inches long and has an "early shape" blade with the Starr Mic-Mac trademark still easily readable on the blade.

As the demand for sticks increased with the formation of more teams and leagues across the country, hockey stick factories appeared in other provinces. Woodsmen in the Windsor area were cutting Nova Scotian yellow birch trees with roots, having them slabbed at a sawmill, and selling them to manufacturers in Ontario who made one-piece hockeys with a natural curve, as the Mi'kmaq and Starr Company had done for years in Nova Scotia.

Homemade Hockeys

Besides those who made hockey sticks for the retail trade, many other Nova Scotians made them either as a hobby, as a favour for a young neighbour, or as a gift for a son or grandson. At a time when there was much less to do than nowadays, and no shame in using a homemade stick, many players made their own sticks, and some made sticks for their team-mates. Early on, a stick was commonly referred to simply as a hurley, or hockey, rather than a hurley stick or hockey stick.

The Goalie's Stick

The goalie got no respect whatsoever for the first century that ice hockey was played. True, he was the only player on the ice who was allowed to stop the puck with his body, but that's not exactly a special privilege. And he had to use the same kind of stick as the other players. For nearly 10 decades, players shot pucks at goalies from all angles, and nobody thought to allow the guardian of the goalmouth a little padding, a face mask, thicker gloves, or even a wider stick.

Hockey team photos taken before 1900 generally reveal the goalie with an ordinary stick, as do the photos of many teams long after that

MIC-MAC HOCKEY STICK — 1906 ad.

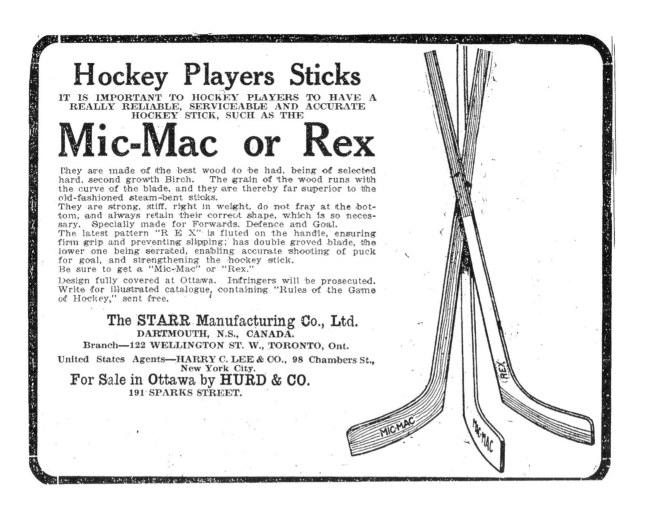

Hockey Players Sticks

IT IS IMPORTANT TO HOCKEY PLAYERS TO HAVE A
REALLY RELIABLE, SERVICEABLE AND ACCURATE
HOCKEY STICK, SUCH AS THE

Mic-Mac or Rex

They are made of the best wood to be had, being of selected
hard, second growth Birch. The grain of the wood runs with
the curve of the blade, and they are thereby far superior to the
old-fashioned steam-bent sticks.

They are strong, stiff, right in weight, do not fray at the bottom, and always retain their correct shape, which is so necessary. Specially made for Forwards. Defence and Goal.

The latest pattern "R E X" is fluted on the handle, ensuring
firm grip and preventing slipping; has double groved blade, the
lower one being serrated, enabling accurate shooting of puck
for goal, and strengthening the hockey stick.

Be sure to get a "Mic-Mac" or "Rex."

Design fully covered at Ottawa. Infringers will be prosecuted.
Write for illustrated catalogue, containing "Rules of the Game
of Hockey," sent free.

The STARR Manufacturing Co., Ltd.
DARTMOUTH, N.S., CANADA.
Branch—122 WELLINGTON ST. W., TORONTO, Ont.

United States Agents—HARRY C. LEE & CO., 98 Chambers St.,
New York City.

For Sale in Ottawa by HURD & CO.
191 SPARKS STREET.

MIC-MAC OR REX HOCKEY STICKS —
1911 Ottawa *Free Press* ad.

date. The Winnipeg Victorias were more aggressive than many other teams in obtaining a better stick for their goalie. As early as 1893, they began adding a piece to the upper surface of the blade, tapering sharply into the handle. This resulted in a wide-on-one-side stick. Teams were generally slow to pick up on this change, but by 1907 team photos were commonly showing a wider stick, often looking like a homemade effort, sometimes more refined. In spite of the availability of the new wide stick, some goalies continued to use a regular hockey stick for some years to come.

By 1906, the Starr Manufacturing Company of Dartmouth was distributing one-piece, handcarved, wide-on-one-side goalie sticks made by Mi'kmaq carvers. These were used by many teams for years to come, and even though a wide-on-both-sides model resembling the stick used today became available in the 1914-15 season, many teams continued to use the wide-on-one-side stick well into the 1920s. Indeed, when the Seattle Hockey Team won the Stanley Cup by beating the Canadiens in 1917, their goalie used the narrower stick as opposed to the new wider stick used by the Montreal goalie. A photo in Brian McFarlane's book on Canadian women's hockey shows the Sudbury women's team still using their favourite wide-on-one-side stick in 1922, seven years after the wider model was available.

The one-piece, wide-on-one-side goalie stick on display at the Windsor Hockey Heritage Centre, used for years in the Annapolis Valley Senior Hockey League by the Wolfville team, has the features of the Mic-Mac brand stick sold by the Starr Skate Company. Sandy Julien, an elderly Mi'kmaq gentleman, recalls the details of his father, Chief Joseph Julien, carving these new, wider goal sticks in his back yard in Millbrook Reserve, near Truro, in the early 1900s. "They were only a little wider, and only on the one side," says Sandy, recalling his father making hockey sticks for a living.

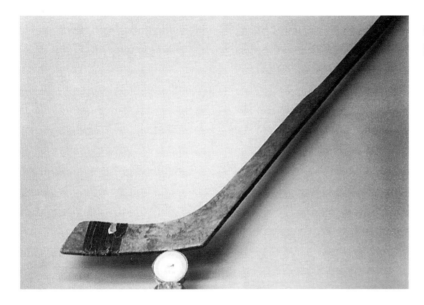

ONE-PIECE GOALIE STICK, 1907 — Resting on a wooden puck.

Garth Vaughan

Laminated Sticks Take Over

In spite of the problems with the bent wood sticks, they remained on the market for four decades, starting in 1888. When the industry in Ontario began to replace them with a new product, hockey sticks took on a new look. The two- and three-piece laminated sticks appeared on the Maritime market in the mid-1930s and became popular almost immediately. First of all, they were new and varnished, whereas previous sticks were plain or oiled and not as attractive. Hockey enthusiasts found the laminated sticks beautiful to look at, expensive to buy, and easy to break. It seems the glue used on early models was not as strong as it might have been, and the sticks had a habit of coming apart exactly where they had been cleverly put together, which made whacking the puck both ineffective and costly.

End of an Era

From 1859, when Boston first sent to Nova Scotia for hockeys made by the Mi'kmaq, until the new flashy laminated sticks appeared in stores, 80 years had passed. The problem with glue on early models was quickly solved with advancing technology, and laminated sticks took over the market. The durable, one-piece, natural-curve Mi'kmaq sticks made in Nova Scotia had been the choice of hockeyists for eight decades, but they were laid aside in barns and attics to become antiques.

The Shape of Sticks

The shape of the hockey stick changed slightly and gradually over the years and chronicled the evolution of the game. The earliest hockey team photos available to us show that the sticks used in the 1880s were still very similar to the original hurley sticks. Subsequent photos through the 1890s and early 1900s reveal a steady trend toward the shape of the stick used today.

Boston sent to Nova Scotia for hockey sticks in 1859.

Montreal sent to Nova Scotia for hockey sticks in 1875.

Kingston sent to Nova Scotia for hockey sticks in 1886.

Hockeys: Past, Present, and Future

Wood was plentiful in all parts of Canada when our national winter sport developed into its mature form. Although wood is a renewable resource, we're finding that it doesn't renew itself quite as fast as we'd like it to, and therefore it is now at a premium and giving way to other materials like aluminum and fibreglass. Millions of wooden sticks have come and gone in the nearly two centuries we've been playing hockey. With Nova Scotia's old recreational game so well established as an international competitive sport, doubtless trillions more hockeys will be made in the years to come. The composition, shape, and design of them should be interesting to observe as ice hockey enters the third century of its life in the season of 2000.

The Starr Company's Acme Club Spring Skates

When ice hockey reached Montreal in 1875, the world-famous Starr skates had only been in existence for 10 years. But in that decade, the magnificent invention of John Forbes and Thomas Batemen had revolutionized ice skating and altered Nova Scotia's amazing new game of ice hockey forever. Forbes was the foreman and Bateman was his assistant at the Starr Manufacturing Company in Dartmouth. They were cognizant of the great demand in their province for better skates, and they had just invented a spring

JOHN FORBES — Inventor of the
Starr self-fastening spring skate.
His 1865 invention revolutionized
skating and ice hockey.

PANS

STARR ACME CLUB SPRING SKATE ON A HIGH-BUTTON BOOT — **The self-fastening spring skate was invented in Dartmouth, Nova Scotia, in 1865 by John Forbes and Thomas Bateman of the Starr Manufacturing Company.**

Garth Vaughan

mechanism which allowed skates to be securely fastened to and quickly removed from boots with the flick of a lever. The predecessors of the new Acme Club spring skates were called stock or block skates and were held to skaters' boots with leather straps and buckles or with rope. The insecurity of stock skates inhibited skaters and hockey players alike, whereas the new spring skates, as they were commonly called, allowed one to achieve greater speed and accuracy, make sharp turns and sudden stops, and change direction without the fear of losing a skate. Consequently, figure skating became more graceful and intricate, and ice hockey became faster and more exciting than ever before.

Boston Bruins
Use
STARR SKATES

"Your skates have stood
the test, and they will
again be part of our
equipment this season."

(Signed) ART ROSS
Manager Boston Bruins

ART ROSS AND THE BOSTON BRUINS
LOVED STARR SKATES — In 1927, the
Boston Bruins decided to use Starr
skates again that season, as stated in
a letter from Art Ross, the manager.

Halifax Herald

Such a compliment from the chief of
the "Boston Bruins," Champions of the
United States section of The National
Hockey League, is a real tribute to Starr
Skates and, in particular, to the Expert
Tube Hockey Skate, the model used
by the Bruins.

*The Expert Tube Hockey Skate is made by
the largest manufacturers of hockey skates in
Canada. Government statistics prove our
claim—and it means that more Starr Hockey
Skates are used in Canada than any other make.*

For 63 years we have been producing skates
unequalled in design, quality and finish—
merit alone has won for them their present
popularity.

*Starr Skates are sold by all good Sporting
Goods and Hardware Dealers. Ask for
Illustrated Catalogue.*

STARR MANUFACTURING COMPANY LIMITED

The Expert Tube Hockey Skate is our
best and latest model. In satin finish,
all styles, $6. Aluminum finish, $5.
Anywhere in Canada

Hitch
Hockey and Skating Boot

made of heavy Box Calf and Mule Hide leathers, light in weight and strong, with or without ankle support and straps over ankle, fleece lined and padded tongues. The most staisfactory Boot made.

Prices For Men's $2.70 to $3.83.
      "   Women's $2.70 to $3.15.
      "   Boys' 1 to 5, $2.48 to $3.15.
      "   Girls' 11 to 2, $2.00 to $2.70.

10 Per cent Discount off for Cash.
PHONE 91-1
Smith Bros.
WINDSOR.

HANTS JOURNAL AD, 1916 — New skates were purchased at the hardware store; hockey boots came from the shoe store. Customers usually put them together the first time, and the shoemaker, the second time!

The Starr Hockey Skate

Having made a great hit with the skatists in 1865, Forbes set out to thrill the hockey players of the province the following year by developing and patenting the Starr hockey skate. While the spring clamping mechanism was exactly the same as was used on the Acme Club skate, the shape and form of the blade was entirely different. Whereas the Acme Club had a long, flat, thin blade, ideal for the long gliding strokes of skatists, the hockey skate had a curved, wider blade with rounded ends to allow for the quick turning and sudden changes in direction so necessary in ice hockey.

In the years that followed, new skate companies emerged in Canada, the U.S., and Europe. However, with superior steel and better clamping devices, Starr skates remained the choice of champions for decades.

The Best Endorsements

Commenting on skates in 1875, the *Encyclopedia Britannica* noted, "many kinds have been invented, but the Acme, first produced in Canada is generally acknowledged as the best." In subsequent years, ice hockey stars continued to endorse Starr skates in newspaper and magazine ads at home and abroad.

The New "Singles" — Screws Included

In the late 1880s, Starr began producing skates which could be permanently applied to the soles and heels of boots with tiny screws. Boots of various styles and quality were sold separately by leather boot companies, and it was left to the purchaser to apply the skates to his or her choice of boots. These nickel-plated skates were commonly called "singles" and quickly became popular with both skatists and hockeyists.

The Ever-Popular Spring Skates

In spite of the fact that Starr produced skates which attached to boots with small screws, the original spring skate, which clamped onto the sole and heel of one's ordinary boots, remained a bestseller into the 1920s. There are lots of seniors today who will tell you that they learned to skate on spring skates.

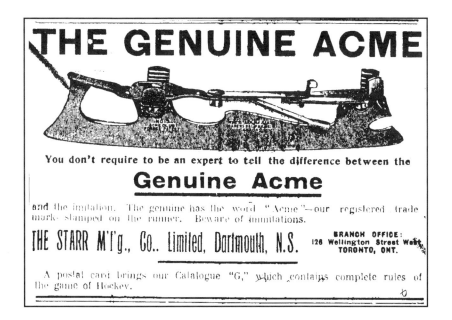

THE GENUINE ACME

You don't require to be an expert to tell the difference between the

Genuine Acme

and the imitation. The genuine has the word "Acme"—our registered trade mark- stamped on the runner. Beware of imitations.

THE STARR M'F'g., Co.. Limited, Dartmouth, N.S.
BRANCH OFFICE:
126 Wellington Street West
TORONTO, ONT.

A postal card brings our Catalogue "G," which contains complete rules of the game of Hockey.

The Puck Stop

Long before goalies got a wider stick than the rest of the team, Starr provided them with a special skate. The company advertised its single-type blades for hockeyists, with or without puck stops. A puck stop was a mountain-shaped elevation on the upper surface of the blade that stopped the puck from going through between the blade and the boot.

THE STARR HOCKEY SKATE, PATENTED IN 1866 — Clamped to boots, the skates had rounded fronts and backs and a curved blade surface for quick turns and sudden stops.

Garth Vaughan

SKATE DISPLAY AT THE STARR FACTORY
— A reminder of a glorious past.

Garth Vaughan

JOHN STARR — His factory
produced nearly 12 million pairs
of Starr skates. They were world
famous for seven decades.

PANS

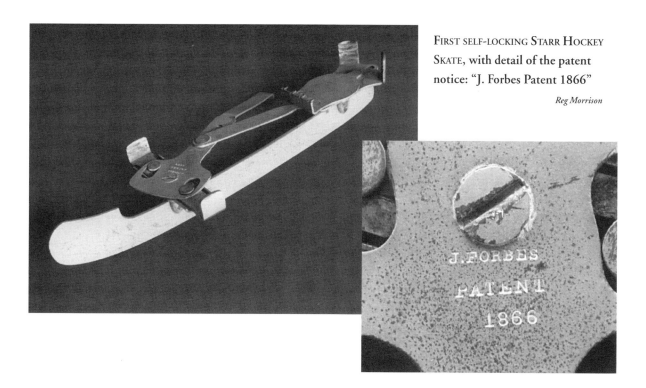

Tube Skates Arrive in 1900

A lightweight tube skate was another step forward in the evolution of hockey skates. The old-fashioned block skate was used for the first 65 years that ice hockey was played. Then came the revolutionary Acme Club spring skate, followed closely in 1866 by the Starr hockey skate, for quicker turns and better mobility. And then, in 1900, Starr produced a skate which was of lighter weight, by virtue of the fact that the supporting struts were made of tubular steel, and the faceplates which screwed onto the sole of the boot were made of very thin steel. The Starr model tube skate had a "star" cut out of the faceplate which unequivocally branded it as a Starr product.

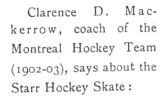

1911 Starr Hockey

Catalogue No. 131.   Quality No. 7.   Price per pair $2.25
"   "   132.   "   " 10.   "   "   3.00
"   "   133.   "   " 11.   "   "   3.75

Sample pattern as above, but with Puck Stop.

Catalogue No. 134.   Quality No. 7.   Price per pair $2.50
"   "   135.   "   " 10.   "   "   3.25
"   "   136.   "   " 11.   "   "   4.00

Made in sizes 9 to 12 inches only.

Please Order by Catalogue Number

Clarence D. Mackerrow, coach of the Montreal Hockey Team (1902-03), says about the Starr Hockey Skate:

"Its a skate that ought to suit anyone playing the game.

I can say it has proved itself the most reliable our Club has used, and I repeat it affords me pleasure to endorse it."

You are entitled to the best—get " Starr."

MONTREAL HOCKEYISTS CHOSE STARR SKATES.

PLAQUE MARKING THE SITE OF THE STARR FACTORY IN DARTMOUTH, NOVA SCOTIA.

Garth Vaughan

Competition and Pressure

Starr skates were favoured by skatists and hockeyists for seven decades. Then, German-made skates, though of inferior quality, flooded the market at lower prices at a time when low prices meant so much. Many Canadian and American companies also emerged and competed well for the market. Retail companies, who were the best customers the Starr Manufacturing Company had, were selling so many Starr skates that they forced down the wholesale price to the point where the margin of profit was so small that Starr could no longer continue in business. The company failed to renew its patent and ceased making skates in 1938.

Starr Manufacturing Company: A Place in Skating and Hockey History

The manufacture of nuts and bolts, screws and nails was the prime purpose of the Starr Manufacturing Company of Dartmouth when it was founded by John Starr, a hardware merchant, in 1861. Although Starr continued and expanded that aspect of its business into the construction of parts for the province's first iron bridges, rail-

ways, and coal cars, it was the company's involvement in the manufacture of the world's finest skates that secured it a place of significance in the history of the evolution of skating and ice hockey.

The Best Steel for the Best Skates

The company was located on Prince Albert Road in Dartmouth in the midst of a busy industrial complex including a molasses factory, lumber mill, grist mill, stone crusher, fish and lobster processing plants, and shipyards. Starr supplied all of these businesses with a variety of products. The company operated on hydro power supplied by the adjacent Shubenacadie Canal and used the best-quality English steel to mass produce high-quality skates.

The Golden Age of Starr Skates

The Starr Manufacturing Company had offices across the harbour in Halifax, as well as in all other major Canadian cities, the U.S.A., Britain, France, Germany, Norway, Russia, and China. At the height of production, the company had as many as 250 employees (often working 14 hours a day) and sold 100,000 pairs of skates a year. The original shares cost $1,000 each, and most years the company paid its shareholders dividends of 15-24 per cent. In 1873, the company celebrated its year-end success by presenting specially gold-plated skates to Lady Dufferin, the wife of Canada's Governor General. In 1876, the company was awarded a Gold Medal of Excellence by the

STARR SKATES AND MCPHERSON BOOTS — McPherson Lightning Hitch hockey boots, made in Ontario, and Starr hockey skates, made in Nova Scotia, were coupled as "the best" companions in the 1920s and 1930s. Hockeyists bought them separately and attached the skate blades with screws or rivets.

Canadian Hockey Year Book (1923)

McPHERSON

PROFESSIONAL HOCKEY BOOTS

The John McPherson Co. Ltd.
HAMILTON, ONT

MAKERS OF THE
FAMOUS LIGHTNING HITCH

STARR "CENTAUR" GOALIE'S SKATE ON A WOODEN PUCK — Note the puck stop and the protective leather pads for the ankle and side of the foot.

Garth Vaughan

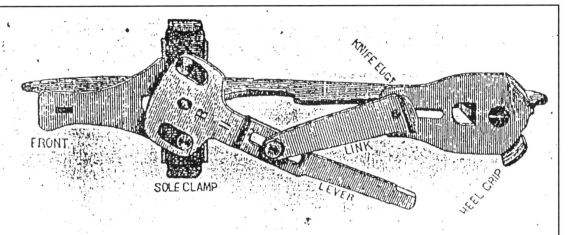

DIRECTIONS FOR FITTING TO BOOTS.

As a rule, when the Skate is closed the sole clamps should be about the thickness of the metal narrower than the sole of the boot, and the heel grip as much smaller than the heel of the boot as will let the knife edge of the link penetrate nearly its full length into the leather.

Loosen the nuts a little with the wrench provided, so that the sole clamps and heel link may be moved easily ; place it upon the boot, with the lever about two-thirds open ; set the edge of the heel link against the front of heel, keeping the Skate pressed forward, and screw the nut up tightly.

Now close the lever to about one-third open, set the sole clamps close against the side of the sole (the runner may be set in the centre of the foot or at one side, to suit the fancy of the wearer), then screw up both nuts securely.

Now open the lever to its full extent, place the skate upon the boot, the sole and heel between their respective fastenings, close the lever and latch it over the runner, the Skate will thus be securely attached to the boot, and may be detached and attached at pleasure, and almost instantly.

☞ In putting on the Skate, press it firmly against the sole of the boot to insure firmness of tread.

If the lever closes too hard, probably too much hold has somewhere been taken.

☞ The soles and heels of boots should be in good condition.

☞ The Skates should be fitted at home, thereby delay at the ice is prevented.

☞ Larger sole clips for fitting extra widths of boots, and duplicates of all parts can always be supplied ; but if any part should break from imperfect material or workmanship the Company will repair such damage gratis.

☞ We warrant all our goods.

THE STARR MANUFACTURING CO.,

HALIFAX, N. S.

The Mic-Mac Hockey
Standard Pattern

Catalogue No. 116.	Quality No. 7.	Price per pair $3.25
" " 117.	" " 10.	" " " 4.00
" " 118.	" " 11.	" " " 4.50

Made the same as above but without puck stop.

Catalogue No. 119.	Quality No. 7.	Price per pair $3.25
" " 120.	" " 10.	" " " 4.00
" " 121.	" " 11.	" " " 4.50

Made only in sizes 10 to 12 inches.

Please Order by Catalogue Number.

12

Here's a good word for a good skate—the "Mic-Mac":

CHICAGO, ILL.,
April 29, 1908.

"I have used your 'Mic-Mac' Skates and find them to be first-class in every respect.

Respectfully yours,
HARRISON B. SILVER
National Medical University,
CHICAGO, ILL."

Starr Skates are different from the others

The Scotia Hockey

Catalogue No. 176.   Price per pair $2.60

We make it in sizes 9½ to 12 inches.

Please Order by Catologue Number

This Hockey Skate was introduced by us in 1908, to meet the demand for a moderate priced welded and tempered and nickeled Hockey Skate. We confidently recommend it as being an excellent skate in every way, and one which will give perfect satisfaction.

Starr Skates have made good.

FROM ACME TO VICTORIA — In 1867, the Starr Company amended the original patent in honour of Confederation and changed the name of the famous skate from the Acme Club to the Victoria Club skate.

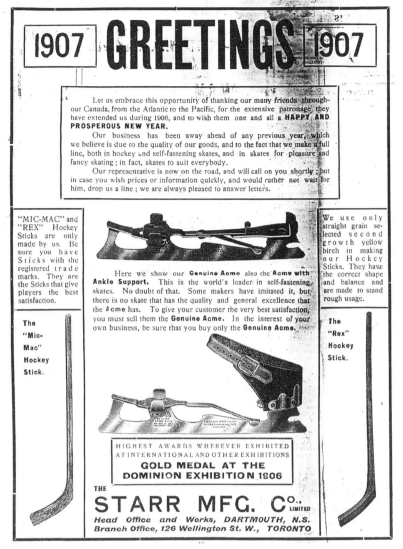

Philadelphia Centennial Exposition. In 1893, Starr Manufacturing won a Gold Medal from the Chicago World Fair, and in the same year was appointed skate maker to King Alfonso of Spain.

Dartmouth: City Of Lakes and Home of the Spring Skate

When the Starr Company was established in 1861, Dartmouth was a small town across the harbour from Halifax, but it has since grown to become a twin city. Dartmouth, now known as the City of Lakes, has no fewer than 23 lakes within its boundaries. As skating and ice hockey were the favourite winter pastimes in Nova Scotia in that era, John Forbes, the company foreman, and his assistant, Thomas Bateman, were used to seeing the lakes swarming with hundreds of skaters of all ages and would have realized the need for better skates.

HOCKEY SKATES

One point about our line which we wish to emphasize, in addition to the unrivalled quality, is the fact that it is a COMPLETE LINE. We have a skate for every need, taste, whim or fancy. In hockey skates we produce several patterns, some of which are here illustrated. We make them in all styles, both with and without puck stops and with plain and flanged runners. The features of our line are well known to every hockey player.

We must apologize for not being able to fill all orders for our new "VELOX" hockey skate promptly. We thought we were making a sufficient quantity to carry us through the season, but, even though we knew the skate's good qualities, we were ourselves surprised at the way in which the public took hold. We have had to put extra effort into turning out the "VELOX" with the result that we are now abreast of our orders.

The "Mic-Mac," standard and featherweight patterns, have lost none of their popularity, and the sales exceed those of any previous season.

Our hockey sticks are popular with all players, because they are made of straight - grain, selected, second - growth, yellow birch, and because they are shaped and balanced perfectly. The reputation they have for durability and playing quality makes them easy sellers.

Our representative is now on the road soliciting orders for 1907-08, and will call on you shortly, but in case you would rather not wait for him, drop us a line; we are always pleased to answer letters.

THE "VELOX"

THE "REGAL"

THE "MIC-MAC"

THE FEATHERWEIGHT "MIC-MAC"

THE "STARR"

THE "CHEBUCTO"

THE "BOY'S"

The "Mic-Mac" Hockey Stick.

The "Rex" Hockey Stick.

HIGHEST AWARDS WHEREVER EXHIBITED
AT INTERNATIONAL AND OTHER EXHIBITIONS
GOLD MEDAL AT
DOMINION EXHIBITION 1906

THE
STARR MFG. CO., LIMITED
Head Office and Works, DARTMOUTH, N.S.
Branch Office, 126 Wellington St. W., TORONTO

The speed at which skating and hockey progressed following the Forbes and Bateman invention was directly proportional to the quality of Starr skates over the conventional stock skates.

In addition to increasing the company's revenues for 70 years, Forbes and Bateman must have experienced great personal satisfaction as they observed the effect of their work worldwide.

The Starr Catalogue

During the 73 years that the Starr Manufacturing Company made skates, it sold more than 11 million pairs. Over the years, 25 new and improved models for both skating and hockey appeared in the company's annual catalogue. The Mic-Mac hockey skate, G.B. (Graceful Beauty) figure skate, and the Ladies' Beaver and Gentleman's Beaver skates, as well as many other models, including bob skates for children, thrilled skaters everywhere.

The catalogue itself was a treasure, for it contained the rules of hockey and drawings of all the many wonderful models of Starr skates available in stores or by mail order from the company office in Halifax. One could also purchase replacement parts and send skates to the factory for sharpening. The Starr catalogue also contained endorsements by famous hockeyists and skatists, was sought by hockey enthusiasts of all ages and was a popular item in most Nova Scotia homes.

Boston Bruins Love Starr Skates

In 1927, Art Ross, manager of the Boston Bruins, endorsed the world-famous Starr skates by stating, "Your skates have stood the test, and they will again be part of our equipment this season." At the time, Starr was still the largest manufacturer of skates in Canada and there were more Starr hockey skates used in Canada than any other make, according to government statistics.

Back to Nuts and Bolts

Today, 135 years later, the famous Starr Manufacturing Company is still in business and producing gigantic nuts and bolts, as it did before it began making the skates which brought world fame. Sadly, a visit to the company today reveals only a small showcase containing a few examples of the many wonderful skates made by the company in its heyday, from 1865 to 1938, when Starr made "Starrs for Stars" or "the Best Skates for the Best Skaters."

Starr Hockey Stick Label

When Canada was a very young nation, and ice hockey was a new game, hockeys were carved by Nova Scotia's Native Mi'kmaq. When the demand for these wonderfully durable one-piece, natural-curve sticks became greater than the Mi'kmaq could supply, the Starr Manufacturing Company began factory production of the same type of sticks and distributed them through their many outlets across the nation. The Starr Company honoured the Mi'kmaq by naming their sticks Mic-Mac and placing their trade mark on each blade, while a paper label on the handle pointed out the features of the sticks:

> We guarantee this stick to be made of thoroughly seasoned selected material, which has been examined and graded by experienced inspectors at the factory. This stick is made in both shape and finish to meet the requirement of most

CRAGG'S RED DOT HOCKEY STICK, c.1920 — In the 1930s, players adopted the habit of reinforcing hockey stick blades with electrical tape. This usually covered the Red Dot and other trademarks branded on the blades.

Garth Vaughan

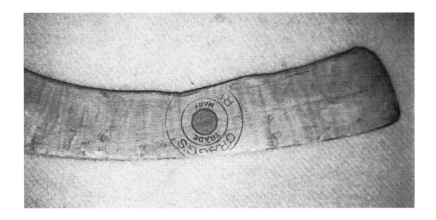

CRAGG'S RED DOT HOCKEY STICK, c.1930 — Tommy Sweet displays the snappy, lightweight bent-wood stick sold by Cragg's Hardware Store in Halifax and on display at the Nova Scotia Sport Heritage Centre in Halifax.

Garth Vaughan

standards and is used and highly appreciated by leading Canadian and American hockey clubs where the highest class only is used.

In the 1920s, it became customary for players to reinforce the blades of their sticks with excessive amounts of black electrical tape, thus concealing the trademarks, but prior to that time, year-end photos of championship teams in Ontario and elsewhere commonly showed players with the Mic-Mac trademark of the Starr company on the blades of their sticks. Starr sticks, like Starr skates, were obviously the choice of Canada's champions.

Saturday Sticks at the Halifax Market

The City Market in Halifax was open on Fridays and Saturdays in the early 1900s, and Tommy Sweet spent a lot of time there with his parents, selling fresh fruit. He recalls the Black community of Preston selling home baking, mayflowers, Christmas wreaths, and blueberries, which they brought to market by horse and wagon on the Dartmouth ferry. The Blacks and the Mi'kmaq of Tufts Cove, near Dartmouth, also sold handmade hockey sticks for 25 and 50 cents each. "No two sticks were exactly alike," said Tom, "You just picked out the one that suited you best." The market would close on Saturdays at 1 p.m., and if the stall-keepers had any sticks left, they would sell them to the kids for 10-15 cents each. "We always liked to make a deal!" recalls Tommy, who adds, "The weather was a lot colder then and it was not uncommon for kids to have games anywhere in the streets, as well as on all the city ponds, as cars were at a minimum back then."

Tommy Sweet with 1865 hockey stick and Starr Rex stick — The 1865 stick was donated to the Nova Scotia Sport Heritage Centre by Mrs. Eva A. Richards of Pictou, N.S. It predates the playing of ice hockey outside the province by 10 years and has been kept in her family home for generations. The Rex brand sticks were made and distributed by the Starr Manufacturing Company from the early 1900s to 1938. Like their Mic-Mac brand sticks, the Rex was a one-piece stick with natural curve made from hockey roots.

Garth Vaughan

The Triumvirate Strikes Again

In 1943, the Canadian Amateur Hockey Association's committee, which had been appointed to investigate the origin of hockey, claimed that Montreal was the site of the origin of goalnets. The same Captain Jim Sutherland, Billy Hewitt, and George Slater, who had bypassed Montreal and Nova Scotia and falsely claimed Kingston to be the birthplace of hockey, once again forgot to look to the east in their search for the facts.

Early Hockey Net, 1908 — The Nova Scotia box net was devised and first used in Halifax on January 6, 1899. It was used in Montreal 11 months later and became so popular that it was soon adopted across Canada. This photo shows a 1908 version of the early hockey net.

PANS

Nova Scotia Box Nets — These nets became popular in Toronto in December, 1899.

HORNBEAM TREE AND LEAVES —
Nova Scotia's early hockey sticks
were made from hornbeam *(Ostrya
Virginiana)* trees. The wood was
known as ironwood because of its
strength and durability. The trunk
and root were used to provide one-
piece sticks with a natural curve.

Garth Vaughan

CHAPTER 8

Mi'kmaq Hockey Stick Makers

Nova Scotia's Mi'kmaq Natives played a role in the evolution of ice hockey. Their contribution was to the game itself as well as its equipment.

A friendly people, the Mi'kmaq greeted each other with "Niqmiq," which means, "my kin friend," a term which gave rise to their tribal name. They travelled about the Maritimes and Maine in search of food and made their own tools, baskets, and clothing. When they settled in communities, they traded their wares for food and clothes, a custom which carried on into the mid-1900s. Long before the province was settled by white people, the Mi'kmaq hunted on ice on bone-blade skates. For enjoyment, they played games together on ice in winter months when their field games could not be enjoyed because of snow. For both hunting and games, they used skates made either from jawbones or shinbones of animals and lashed them to their larrigans or mocassins with strips of rawhide.

Oochamkunutk and Alchamadijik

The Mi'kmaq had their own stickball game which they called Oochamkunutk. Later, when they joined white people in playing hurley-on-ice, they would contribute their own knowledge of ice play to the development of ice hockey. The Mi'kmaq name for the new game of hurley-on-ice was Alchamadijik.

Alder Sticks for Kids, Hornbeam for Adults

Native children often made their own sticks from stalks of alder trees, which had a natural hockey-stick shape to begin with. By trimming alders down to the appropriate size with their parents' draw

ENCAMPMENT AT EVANGELINE BEACH, KING'S COUNTY, N. S., 1907 — Nova Scotia's Natives moved about in search of food and shelter. They made and peddled baskets, tools, furniture, and hockey sticks in various communities. This group was settled on the shores of Minas Basin, near Windsor. Note apple baskets in foreground, used in the Annapolis Valley apple industry.

Aileen Bishop

knives, they began their own careers as master carvers, which was a trait of the Mi'kmaq, and a necessity in providing their homes, furniture, and tools. Their hunting bows and handles for shovels, axes, and picks were daily necessities that required them to carve wood. For tough jobs, they chose tough wood, and one of the strongest and most durable was the hornbeam tree, which is native to the province. Hornbeam was often called ironwood, because of its nature, and stinkwood because of its odour.

Craftsmen of the Millbrook Reserve

At least three generations of Mi'kmaq carvers in the Cope family of Millbrook, Colchester County, near Truro, Nova Scotia, carved sticks for hurley and hockey. Raymond Cope and his good friend and neighbour Alexander Julien, a fellow Mi'kmaq, have lived, played, and worked together on the Millbrook Reserve since childhood. They both know the carving trade well and recall their parents and grandparents making a living carving handles, bows, and hockey sticks. They also know of sticks being made by Natives on other reserves. The Mi'kmaq were also skilled at making furniture and baskets, which they used in their own homes and sold as well.

MI'KMAQ LOVE ICE HOCKEY — Raymond Cope and Sandy Julien with a square saw, used by Native hockey stick makers. Raymond and Sandy have played hockey since childhood. They stuck with old-timers hockey in the Truro area for years and "only recently" hung up their skates. As children, they made their own cherry-wood pucks, sticks, and moose skin shin guards.

Garth Vaughan

Hockey Roots

When Raymond and Sandy speak of their parents, Alex Cope and Joe Julien, as hockey-stick makers, they tell how their fathers and friends would set off for the woods with horse and wagon in the fall, long before the snow arrived, in search of hockey roots. A substantial tree, either hornbeam or yellow birch, with exposed roots the shape of a hockey stick was the object of their search, and the Mi'kmaq carvers called such trees "hockey roots." Arriving in the woods, they would tie their horse and go in different directions looking for hockey roots. Once a suitable root was identified, the earth was dug away from it and the root was chopped to come away with the trunk of the tree.

RAYMOND COPE, MI'KMAQ HOCKEYIST AND CARVER — Raymond first played hockey with fellow Mi'kmaq on the Millbrook Reserve, then in the Truro District League. In the sunset of his hockey career he played with old-timers teams where he made the all stars seven years in a row. He remembers his father making hockey sticks for a living.

Helena Smith

RAYMOND COPE — **Old-timer hockeyist.**

Raymond Cope

Shaping the Sticks

Finding and gathering the hockey roots was the first stage of the process. Next came the artistic part, uniformly shaping the actual sticks.

In later years the hockey roots were taken to a mill and cut lengthwise into slabs. Back home, a pattern of a hockey stick was laid on a slab and the stick was drawn on the surface. Often, two or three sticks could be cut from a slab, and of course several slabs were obtained from each tree, so that any tree might offer up as many as a dozen hockey sticks. Then came the job of cutting out the sticks from the slabs. This was done with an ingenious two-handsaw

which they called a square-saw, made by the craftsmen from metal and wood. (After the gramophone had been invented and was around for awhile, the task of making saw blades became easier, for the metal springs from discarded gramophones made ideal strong saw blades.) With the basic shape of the sticks established, they were then hung on racks made of thin poles and suspended by wires from the kitchen ceiling over the stove. The water would gradually dry out of the wood, making the sticks ideal for carving into the final form with drawknives and crooked-knives. After a slight curve was carved into the blade, establishing it as left or right, the sticks were sandpapered and the job was complete.

Off to Market

Many of the sticks were used locally by hockey players in the Truro area, and others were bundled in dozens and shipped by train to Halifax to Phinney's Ltd., or Creighton's Ltd., as well as other sport or hardware stores. Some were, in turn, shipped off to the hockey trade in other provinces.

"Old Joe" Cope

An older relative of Raymond Cope was a much respected gentleman who was affectionately known as "Old Joe" Cope. Joe was a boxer and taught many of the children on the reserve to spar. Indeed, Raymond still has a punching bag hanging in his basement above his carving horse and uses both of them regularly in his seventh decade. Joe played the fiddle and flute, wrote to the Halifax papers on occasion in defence of his fellow man, and was interested in discussing things historic with almost anyone. In 1942, when claims were being made in Ontario that hockey originated there, Old Joe Cope was one of two Nova Scotians who spoke out publicly to point out that hockey had been played in Nova Scotia first. Joe had been a woodcarver all his life, and he said that he personally had made some of the sticks that were sent to Ontario for the first games played there. Joe had played hockey with the military and locals on the Dartmouth lakes and certainly had made more than his share of hockey sticks.

The Price of the Hockey Stick

The value of money was far different then, and it is difficult for us to equate prices then and now, but it is interesting to know that, in the early 1900s, sticks retailed for as little as 25 cents each, and the best quality handcarved Mic-Mac brand sticks sold for $4.50 per dozen in team lots in the Eaton's catalogue. One is left wondering what the master carvers were paid for their efforts in supplying the hockey sticks with which our national winter sport was shaped in those times. Sandy Julien and Ray Cope can tell us all about the method of making the sticks, but neither has any idea what their fathers and friends got paid by the distributors for their efforts. Whatever their fathers were paid, it must have been important to them, because the carving went on year after year. The Mi'kmaq craftsmen supplied Canada's hockey sticks in the early days of the evolution of ice hockey and were put out of a job in the 1930s when factory-made laminated sticks came on the market at a cost of $1.35 each.

That was twice the price of a 75-cent Mi'kmaq stick in Canada's hardware stores at the time. But the factory-made sticks were new, varnished, shiny, and in great demand regardless of the cost. Jim Wilcox of Windsor, who began working in his father's hardware store at the time that laminated sticks first appeared, recalls them outselling the Mi'kmaq sticks which were left standing, unwanted, until they changed colour with age. For a century, the handmade Mi'kmaq sticks had served their purpose. They were inevitably replaced with the modern two-piece laminated sticks, even if these did cost double the price and usually broke apart at the glued joint before they had scored many goals.

MARLBOROS, TORONTO OHA SENIOR CHAMPIONS, 1905 — OHA champions preferred Mic-Mac sticks, made in Nova Scotia, and proudly displayed them in year-end team photos.

Canadian Hockey Yearbook (1923)

Childhood Hockey at the Millbrook Reserve

Reminiscing about their fun playing hockey on the frozen river on the Millbrook Reserve in their youth, Ray and Sandy tell of the importance of picking a spot on the ice well away from the unfrozen area where the water was running, not so much for the fear of falling in, as for the danger of losing their pucks. "We used black cherry wood pucks, and if the goalie didn't stop them, they'd go in the water and float away!" Why black cherry and not spruce, maple, or birch? The boys point out that cherry bark shrinks more than the wood and therefore stays in place and is easy to see against ice and snow because of its rich, dark colouring. "Cherry makes a better puck. It's just that simple!" says Sandy. Their sticks were sometimes made by their fathers, but more often they were alder wood sticks which they shaped themselves. And what about protective equipment? "The most important thing was having good pads for the goalie, and we made our own out of moose hide," Sandy says. Ray points out, "Our fathers always had moose skins hanging around, and they were thick and strong, and we'd cut them to fit the goalie's legs and tie them on him. We made his chest protector the same way." And Sandy adds, "We just used magazines for our own shin pads. One of the guys had a *True Story* magazine one time and we took it and were reading it and teasing him for having it." Then Raymond recalls, "One of the guys used an aluminum tea kettle to make his own cup one time and we all thought that was pretty funny!"

Chief Frank Toney's Family Industry

Frank Toney, a much respected Native craftsman, was chief of the Mi'kmaq reserve of King's County in the Annapolis Valley in the 1920s and 1930s and made hockey sticks for a living. His wife, Mary Lucy, was an expert basket weaver, and they each passed their crafts on to their children, who worked with them earning a living.

Young, Small, Straight Trees

Unlike the Mi'kmaq of Millbrook who used larger trees, each of which yielded several sticks, Frank chose smaller second-growth trees that were easier to handle.

A Job after School

The two oldest boys, Tom and Pat, helped Frank by going to the woods after school to look for hockey roots, which were young yellow birch trees with exposed roots in the natural shape of a hockey stick. The straight trees were harvested, root and all, by digging out the root, cutting down the trees, and loading them on their horse-drawn

NOEL AND RITA SMITH WITH THEIR
MAGNIFICENT APPLE BASKETS —
Rita learned the art of basket
weaving from her mother, and
she remembers that her father,
Chief Frank Toney, made hockey
sticks from hockey roots.

Garth Vaughan

wagon (or sleigh, if there was snow on the ground). Heading back
home with axe and shovel, work complete, the next part of their job
was to arrange the hockey roots on racks for drying before they
would help their father shape them into hockey sticks with saws,
drawknives, and sandpaper.

Fussy Mary Lucy

For basket weaving, Mary Lucy used ash, because it split nicely into
flat, smooth strips, ideal for working into basket shapes. Ash trees
were tested for quality by making a nick in the bark and pulling it.
If it tore easily and stripped straight down without difficulty, it
meant that the wood of that tree would respond the same way to

preparation for basket strips. Apple baskets were always needed in the Annapolis Valley for harvesting the apples, most of which were shipped out of Windsor for the British market. Then again, before the age of plastic, women always needed clothes baskets and shopping baskets, so there was a great demand for Mary Lucy's products just as there was for Chief Frank's hockey sticks.

Door-to-Door Service

When sticks and baskets were abundant, Frank and Mary Lucy and one or more of the children would travel with their bundles by train to nearby towns to sell them to the residents. As Natives, they were allowed to travel for part fare on the Dominion Atlantic Railway. The baskets were bundled by tying the handles together and wrapping several such bundles into a large cloth sheet with the corners tied. Mary Lucy would sling a couple of these over her shoulder, as would Frank, who also carried a bundle of hockey sticks. They would move along the town's streets from house to house, showing their pieces and making sales.

Treasures in Falmouth Barns

In the farming area of Falmouth, across the river from Windsor, they also walked for great distances on country roads selling to farmers. Young Rita frequently went along and recalls that Mary Lucy would pin her to her skirt so she couldn't wander off while she was busy with a customer. Rita, who learned her mother's craft well, became an excellent basket weaver and has been the subject of a television documentary. The baskets made by Rita and her husband, Noel Smith, of Bishopville, near Hantsport, were always in great demand. Now since they've retired, their apple baskets in particular have become collectors' items. And what about Frank's hockeys? One at least, in excellent condition, has been found and forms a part of the collection at the Windsor Hockey Heritage Centre. We're still looking for more of those treasures in Falmouth barns!

Many Valley residents recall Chief Frank Toney and his family peddling their wares from door to door in the 1920s and 1930s. Indeed, many still proudly possess baskets, both ornamental and functional, made by these skilful artists.

In making hockey sticks for a living, Frank Toney at the Cambridge Reserve in Kings County joined other Native craftsmen from Tufts Cove, near Halifax and Dartmouth, Pictou Landing, and the Millbrook Reserve, near Truro, in supplying not only local hockey

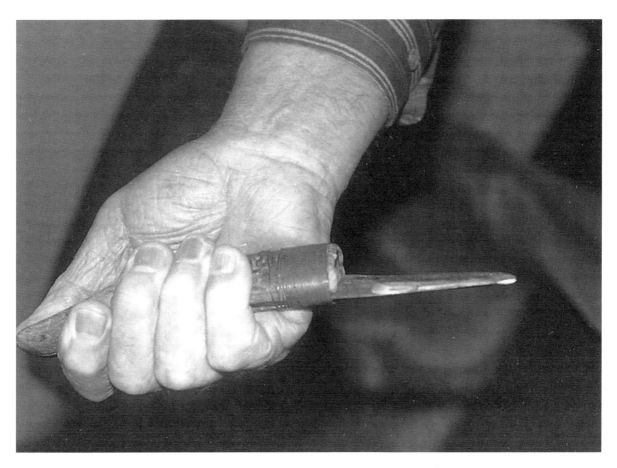

MI'KMAQ CROOKED-KNIFE.

Garth Vaughan

players with their sticks, but also supplying the rest of the Canadian market. For thousands of their fine products were shipped off to other provinces for hockey players who loved their sticks every bit as much as the Nova Scotian hockeyists.

Pirate Hockey Sticks

The labels on a couple of the sticks in a photo of the Ladies Seminary Hockey Team of Acadia University taken in 1923, when subjected to a large magnifying glass, are seen to read, "Pirate Hockey Stick, made by the Pirate Hockey Stick Company, Wolfville, N.S." Local historians Gordie Hansford and Roy Murphy recalled not only the details of the company but also the owner and employees as well as their techniques and markets!

Housed in a red-ochre-coloured building the size of a modern double garage near the DAR Station, overlooking Cape Blomidon and the Minas Basin, the Pirate Hockey Stick Company was owned by Mr. Fred Rand, a local pharmacist and hockey enthusiast. The staff was made up of local wood craftsmen, including Chief Frank

MI'KMAQ DRAWKNIFE AND CROOKED-KNIFE — Used in shaping the famous one-piece hockey sticks from the early 1800s to the 1930s.

Garth Vaughan

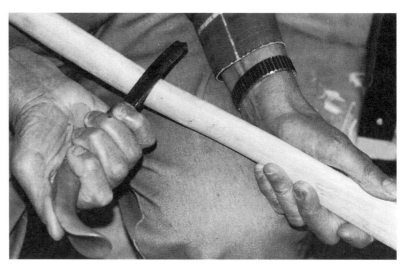

HOCKEY STICK MADE BY PIRATE
HOCKEY STICK COMPANY OF
WOLFVILLE, N.S. — One-piece
sticks made in Wolfville from
hockey roots in the 1920s by
Nova Scotia Natives.

Larry Keddy

Toney and his sons Tom and Pat, who previously made sticks at home. The birch trees used to carve the sticks were supplied by Mi'kmaq woodsmen from nearby Cambridge and Bishopville.

The sticks were hand-carved in the traditional Mi'kmaq method, using crooked-knives and drawknives, and allowed to dry in a large yard filled with drying racks. There, one could view hundreds of hockey sticks in the rough, out to dry in the breezes flowing in from the Bay of Fundy. When dry, they would be sandpapered before having the Pirate Hockey Stick label applied and being sent to market.

Kentville Wildcats Use Pirate Hockey Sticks

Many of the sticks were sold through local hardware stores to players in Annapolis Valley leagues. The many teams of Acadia University and Horton Academy, the towns of Wolfville and Kentville, plus a myriad of other local hockey players supported the Pirate Hockey Stick Company. Other sticks were bundled and shipped to Halifax on the Dominion Atlantic Railway for distribution elsewhere in Canada and abroad.

One of the biggest shippers of the locally made sticks was Creighton's, owned and operated by James George Andrew Creighton of Halifax, who was a relative of the James George Aylwin Creighton who took ice hockey to Montreal from Nova Scotia.

The small but effective Pirate Hockey Stick Company operated for several years in the 1920s but did not rebuild following a fire which completely destroyed the factory, thus leaving the industry to bigger manufacturers elsewhere.

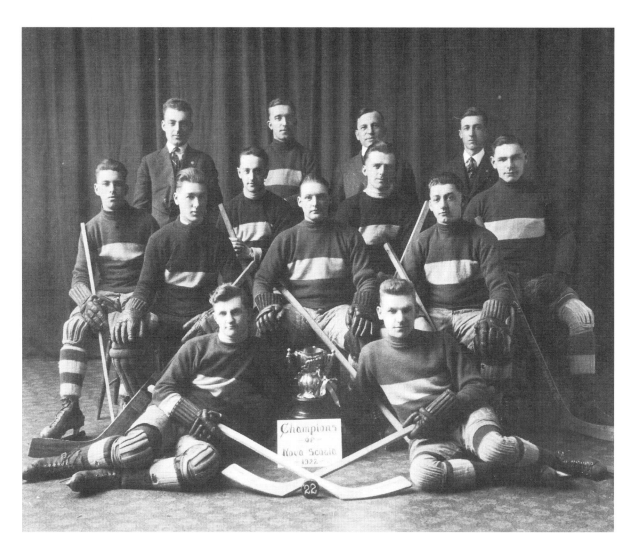

WINDSOR HOCKEY TEAM, NOVA SCOTIA CHAMPIONS, 1922 — Proud winners of local, regional, and provincial titles, these stalwarts regularly brought the silver back to their home town. Back row: G. Robertson, manager; Frank Clark, forward; A.E. Andrew, president; Cliff Smith, secretary; middle row: S. MacDonald, right defence; G. Smith, goal; J. Hughes, forward; F. Poole (captain), forward; front row: C. Wigmore, left defence; Vic McCann, defence; E. Mosher, forward; Bill Singer, forward; J. MacDonald, forward.

Carrie McCann

CHAPTER 9
Praise, Medallions, and Trophies

Words of praise from family, fans, and team-mates is all that losers have to remind them of the series, besides their bruises and disappointment. In the beginning, with the exception of the disappointment, that's all there was for winners as well. Then along came medallions, which served to distinguish champions for some years, until trophies appeared on the scene in the 1890s.

A strange stipulation was included in the rules concerning the awarding of Canada's first trophies which led to confusion and disappointment. The rule stated that any team good enough to win the trophy three years in a row could keep it. While it's highly unlikely for that to happen these days, nevertheless it did happen early on.

In 1893, the Montreal Amateur Athletic Association won the Amateur Hockey Association of Canada Trophy for the third consecutive year and became permanent owners. It was a glorious trophy that dwarfed the newly presented Stanley Challenge Trophy. The ruling effectively took the trophy out of circulation. What a waste!

In the Maritimes, an equally impressive Starr Trophy was similarly captured by the Moncton Victorias in 1907, 1908, 1909, and the team rightfully took permanent possession. Some years later, Moncton graciously put it back in circulation, excluding the three-win clause.

In Windsor, Nova Scotia, the fans raised money for the beautiful silver Citizens' Trophy in 1899. The first trophy used in the Town League, it was won the first three years by the Avonians; thus the citizens lost the trophy to the home of the team captain for 80 years. Recently, through the kindness of the family, it has been donated for display in the museum of the Windsor Hockey Heritage Society.

THE STANLEY CUP REFUSED! — The first team to win the Lord Stanley Challenge Trophy didn't want it. The Montreal Amateur Athletic Association Hockey Club had just won the large and glorious Canadian Amateur Hockey Association trophy for the third consecutive time, and in so doing became owners. What a prize! On the other hand, and in stark contrast, the newly presented $7^1/_2$"-high Stanley rose bowl was to remain in circulation regardless of multiple wins, and the Montreal players didn't like that. They chose to ignore it and would not accept it. One year later, following a series of tough negotiations, a shiny black-lacquered wooden base with a silver plaque containing the names of each of the Montreal Hockey Club players was added to the cup. This made the difference for the winners, who then decided to accept it. The trophy soon became known as the Stanley Cup, which is now identified as the most coveted hockey trophy in North America.

Medallions Hard to Find

The medallions of yesteryear are not in great evidence across the country. Currently, medallions are passed out in great numbers at many sporting events, but those won by championship teams before the age of trophies are collector's items, difficult to find.

The Starr Hockey Trophy

When the Starr Trophy was donated to the newly formed Halifax Hockey League for competition in 1897, the Halifax *Herald* described it as "a cup of appropriate design . . . and one of the finest objects which athletic organizations have had to contend for in the lower provinces and possibly throughout the Dominion . . . in keeping with the Starr company's reputation of being the manufacturer of some of the best goods in the world." At the time, the Starr Manufacturing Company of Dartmouth employed more than 200 workmen who worked 14 hours a day producing the finest skates in the world. Stockholders were getting 15 per cent interest on their investments, and more than 100,000 pairs of the popular Starr skates were sold annually across Canada and the U.S. as well as in Europe and Asia.

The Citizens' Trophy, 1900 — Windsor, a town of 2000 residents, had four senior teams competing annually for this trophy, which was donated by the town's grateful fans. It is on display at the Windsor Hockey Heritage Centre.

WHHC

The Starr Trophy — Donated by the Starr Manufacturing Company for amateur ice hockey competition in 1897, the glorious Starr Trophy was used in the Halifax Hockey League until 1904, when it became the symbol of Maritime Senior Hockey League supremacy. At the time there was no such thing as a "professional" hockey player, and both the Stanley and Starr trophies were used to signify amateur excellence in ice hockey. The Stanley Cup cost the Governor General $48.66 and was simply a silver rose bowl that was not designed as a challenge trophy. The Starr Trophy, by contrast, was commissioned and designed specifically as a hockey championship trophy at great expense. One of the most elegant and glorious trophies in all of Canada, the cost of the Starr Trophy was never revealed by the makers of the Starr skates which had revolutionized ice hockey. At the time these trophies were donated by Lord Stanley and the Starr Manufacturing Company, Quebec and Ontario had taken the lead in the development of Canada's new game. Originating in Nova Scotia, ice hockey had just reached British Columbia on its introductory trip across the nation when these two famous trophies appeared.

NSSHC

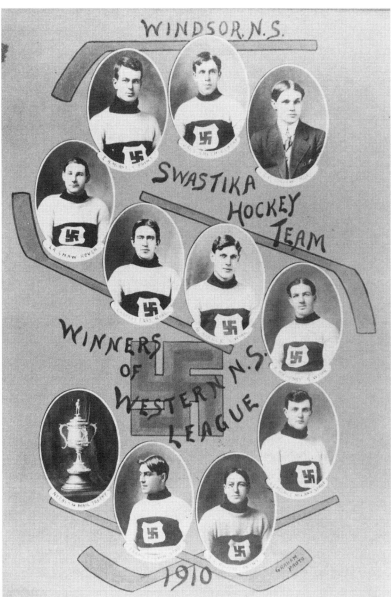

The company directors were proud of their accomplishments and naturally wanted to support their customers, the hockey players, by presenting them with this elegant trophy.

Starr Trophy Not Surpassed

When the Starr Trophy first appeared for public viewing in the window at Sarre's Rink, the *Acadian Recorder* reported, "It has excited the admiration of the public and is a beautiful piece of workmanship. It is probably not surpassed in Canada as a trophy for hockey clubs, as those who have seen the Stanley Cup say that it does not excel this trophy in beauty and magnificence."

The original Starr Trophy, which stands over three feet high, is quite likely the most elegant and magnificent-looking hockey trophy in Canada. Designed especially as a hockey trophy, the upper portion lifts off to reveal a gold-lined cup portion. An engraving on its surface depicts a game in progress in which the players have no gloves, the goalie uses an ordinary stick, and the goalposts have no net. Statues of two individual hockey players on side pedestals symbolize competitive teams, and, on top, a standing figure holding an oak-leaf wreath overhead symbolizes the victor. Sterling silver crossed hockeys, a puck, and skate blades indicate the equipment used to play the game. By comparison, the Stanley Cup was a rose bowl, 7$^1/_2$" high, designed to be used in one's home to display roses, and was purchased in England at a cost of $48.66. The multiple rings and additional height of the Stanley Cup have been added in the years since Lord Stanley first donated it for use as an amateur hockey trophy in Ontario, as the Starr Trophy was presented for amateur use in Halifax. The Starr Manufacturing Company, whose skates revolutionized ice skating as well as hockey, never revealed the cost of the magnificent custom-made Starr Trophy.

NOVA SCOTIA SENIOR CHAMPIONSHIP TROPHY, 1904 — The Nova Scotian box net originated in 1899, and the format displayed on the trophy is one of the earliest used in the game of ice hockey. In the early 1900s, the Harold A. Wilson sporting goods store in Toronto was selling these nets for "$15.00 pair, complete."

PANS

The Halifax Hockey League

The Halifax Wanderers were first to win the most elegant silver hockey trophy ever created and used in the country to this day. The following year the Crescents won it, and these two teams won it in alternate years until the 1904-05 season, when the trophy came to be used in the newly formed Maritime Senior Hockey League.

Maritime Senior Championship

The valuable and much coveted piece of silverware was first won in Maritime Senior competition by the Amherst Ramblers, who lost out to New Glasgow the following 1905-06 season.

Losers, Weepers

The Moncton Victorias then won the trophy three years in a row and, having become the permanent owners of the glorious Starr Trophy, took it out of circulation in 1909.

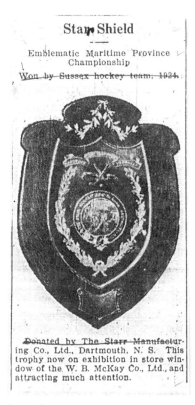

Starr Shield

Emblematic Maritime Province Championship

Won by Sussex hockey team, 1924.

Donated by The Starr Manufacturing Co., Ltd., Dartmouth, N. S. This trophy now on exhibition in store window of the W. B. McKay Co., Ltd., and attracting much attention.

STARR SHIELD.

Bill Bailey

The Starr Shield

The Starr Manufacturing Company then donated a new Starr trophy in the form of a very large silver shield, beautifully mounted on a polished wooden plaque, with space on the periphery for smaller shields which recognized the yearly winners.

When the Maritime Starr Shield was destroyed by fire in 1947, Moncton graciously returned the original Starr Trophy to the Maritime Amateur Hockey Association (MAHA) for competition once again.

Over the years, various outstanding Maritime hockey teams, having won their local senior division title, went on to defeat the winners of other divisions, thus capturing the provincial title as well, before pressing on to become senior hockey champions of the Maritime Provinces.

LORD STANLEY, GOVERNOR GENERAL OF CANADA, **from 1888 to 1893** — "Professionalism" in ice hockey emerged on centre stage in 1907, when the trophy which the Governor General had donated for "amateur" competition, as the Dominion Championship Trophy, became the world-famous Stanley Cup. The 48-year-old Lord Stanley, his wife, and their family of two daughters and eight sons all became interested in the game of ice hockey. His favourite hockey team, Ottawa's Rideau Hall Rebels, with his sons Arthur and Edward as players, did much to popularize the new game in Ontario. During their five-year stay in Canada, the Stanley family witnessed the development of ice hockey in Ontario and its introduction to Western Canada. When they left Canada to return to England in 1893, the game was being played in British Columbia, and wooden rinks were being constructed in cities and towns from coast to coast. In 1895, Lord Stanley captained a team that challenged the Royal Family to a game of ice hockey on an outdoor rink at Buckingham Palace. Four of his sons, including Arthur and Edward, who had played in Canada, were members of his team on that occasion.

Brian McFarlane

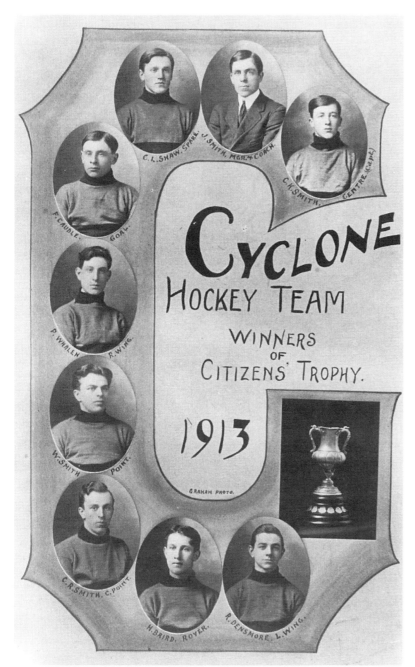

CYCLONE HOCKEY TEAM
WINNERS OF CITIZENS' TROPHY.
1913

GRAHAM PHOTO.

C.L.SHAW, SPARE. J.SMITH, MGR.& COACH. C.K.SMITH, CENTRE (CAPT.)

F.CAUDLE, GOAL.

P.WHALEN, R.WING.

W.SMITH, POINT.

C.R.SMITH, C.POINT.

H.BAIRD, ROVER. R.DENSMORE, L.WING.

WINDSOR'S CYCLONE HOCKEY TEAM — In 1913 the Cyclones had to contend with the Swastikas, the Socials, and King's College for the Citizen's Trophy of the Town League.

Howard Dill

Prizes for the Winners

Each year, in addition to the honour of winning the Starr Trophy, members of the championship team also benefited by being presented by the Starr Manufacturing Company with a new pair of Starr skates to use the following season. In addition, the MAHA executive presented each of the winning players with a heavy wool coat sweater in the team colours. These sweaters were much in vogue at the time and would indeed be coveted by the newly crowned hockey champions of the Maritimes. Each of the champion players

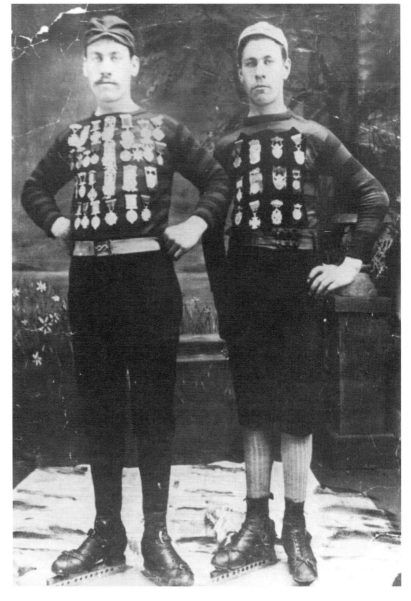

traditionally received a gift of appreciation from their local town fans. A demitasse displaying a picture of the Starr Trophy, presented to members of the New Glasgow team, winners of the trophy in 1906, is presently on display at the Windsor Hockey Heritage Centre.

Starr Trophy for Windsor's Stars

The Windsor Maple Leafs won the Maritime title in the 1963-64 season and were judged to be the most successful team in Nova Scotia hockey history and the finest senior hockey team ever to take to the ice in the Maritimes.

THE SYDNEY MILLIONAIRES WITH THE STARR TROPHY, 1913 — Erroneously referred to as the "Sydney Miners" in Dan Diamond's *The Official National Hockey League Stanley Cup Centennial Book,* the Millionaires challenged the Quebec Bulldogs for the Stanley Cup in 1913, four years before the NHL was formed, at a time when amateurs were still permitted to mount challenges. In 1900, the Halifax Crescents had challenged the Montreal Shamrocks for the amateur Dominion Hockey Challenge Cup, which is what Lord Stanley had intended the cup to be: an award for victory in amateur hockey. In the 1906-07 season, New Glasgow challenged the Montreal Wanderers for the trophy. All of the teams from Nova Scotia lost their bid for the big one, but then again, so have many others. The players are wearing coat sweaters presented annually to the Maritime Champions by the MAHA.

Canadian Hockey Year Book (1923)

BOY SCOUTS HOCKEY TEAM, 1912-13 — The youth of the town sponsored a league and vied for the Windsor Tribune Trophy (with ribbons). They wore single-blade skates and used their hockeys until the blades were worn round. Young Frank Poole (front) was wearing a brand-new pair of hockey gloves, while Vic McCann and Ross Cochran wore unpadded work gloves. All players wore lightweight unpadded short trousers that had only recently replaced over-the-knee knickers. Clyde Curry, the goalie, has a wide-on-one-side stick, which had only been available since the early 1900s.

Aubrey McCann

Maritime Senior teams challenged for the Starr Trophy from 1904 until the league folded in 1965. That was the year that Nova Scotia's provincial archivist, C.Bruce Fergusson, wrote his account of Thomas Chandler Haliburton's description of hurley being played on Windsor's Long Pond around 1800. Shortly thereafter, Judge J. Elliott Hudson, president of the MAHA, personally delivered the Starr Trophy to Windsor for safekeeping and permanent possession. The trophy is now on display in the Windsor Hockey Heritage Centre.

The Avonians and the Citizens'
Trophy, 1900 — Hockey fans of
Windsor donated the Citizens'
Trophy for senior competition.
No less than four teams of town
players battled for the cup annually.

Peter MacKinnon

Annapolis Valley League
champions — The Windsor Maple
Leafs frequently won the Annapolis
Valley Senior Hockey title. Team
Captain Harry Ettinger receives the
trophy from Albert Levy, president
of the Valley League, while Bob
Huggins does the play-by-play for
the Evangeline Broadcasting
Company.

Marguerite Ettinger

Bathurst Papermakers, Winners of the Starr Trophy (shield), 1929 — Players received individual trophies from the citizens of Bathurst, New Brunswick, coat sweaters in team colours from the MAHA, and new skates from the Starr Manufacturing Company in recognition of their achievement.

City of Bathurst

CHAPTER 10

Hockey in the Early 1900s

In a way, games of amateur hockey played after 1900 in the average Canadian town were different from those played before. Hockey's second period had begun. People in all provinces had been introduced to the game, and western innovations had found their way back east. The game was being called hockey instead of ice hockey. Rules had been standardized, and the game was being played pretty much the same in all parts of the country. Leagues were forming to pit town against town, and protective equipment was being developed to match the increased roughness of the game. Teams were travelling by horse and sleigh to play in new covered rinks in adjacent towns. Fans were buying tickets on hockey pools and getting more deeply interested in the game with each successive season.

An Exciting Future Ahead

Although it would be 33 years before Foster Hewitt began greeting his radio audience with "Hello Canada, and hockey fans in the United States and Newfoundland," hockey's popularity was growing quickly. Hockey night in Canada had truly arrived and was here to stay! The amount of hockey activity in small Canadian towns was unbelievable, and Windsor was a perfect example of the phenomenon. In 1900, the hockey fans of Windsor (a town of barely 2000 people) were watching faithfully as no fewer than four senior teams, consisting entirely of local amateur players, battled for the Citizens' Trophy. The Avonians, Elgraves, Resolutes, and King's College vied for senior hockey supremacy in the town. The championship offered the privilege of a year's possession of the coveted silver Citizens' Trophy, which had been paid for and presented by their wonderfully faithful fans.

NEW BRICK BUILDINGS, WATER
STREET, WINDSOR, C. 1910 —
Following a fire which destroyed
the town's many wooden structures
in 1897, the town was completely
rebuilt. The business district was
replaced with fine sandstone and
brick buildings, some of which
still serve the town.

Postcard, Valentine and Sons

In Love . . . with Hockey!

If interest in playing outdoor sports was as high in Windsor in 1800
as it was in 1900, it's no wonder ice hockey originated here. Following a tragic fire which effectively destroyed the town in 1897, the
homes and buildings had been quickly rebuilt by 1900, including
the covered rink, one of the first to be erected in the country (in
1870). Its replacement was a grand, spruce-shingled structure with
a fancy cupola rising high over the front door. The Canadian Ensign,
mounted above all, proudly flew on all days that ice conditions were
suitable for skating. All ice was "natural" ice in those days, and skat-

ing depended on the temperature being low enough to freeze a new sheet at least once a day. The flying Ensign was a signal to the town that the rink was operating on any given day. "The flag's up!" was the message that circulated through the school and town as soon as anybody saw it flying. There would be skating that afternoon and, better still, there would be hockey that night.

Pond Hockey – A Must

Even though the town was blessed by having a covered rink, ice hockey continued to be played and skating went on all over town on Windsor's many ponds. Bonfires were lit both in the afternoons and evenings to warm eager adults and children seeking to try their skills at one of the very few winter athletic activities of the day.

KING'S COLLEGE HOCKEY TEAM, 1920, WINDSOR — **Most players used hockey gloves, but some preferred kid gloves. The goalie still used his favourite wide-on-one-side stick, six years after the wide-on-both-sides stick was available.**

King's-Edgehill School

WINDSOR SCOUTS JUNIOR
HOCKEY TEAM, 1915 — Back row:
G. Maxner, J. Huges. Middle row:
A. Smith, G. Smith, C. Bissett.
Front row: W. Singer, F. Mounce.
This team travelled to Wolfville,
a distance of 18 miles, by horse
and sleigh to play games. Mr.
Charles "Charlie" Dill would
tend his team during the game
and then drive the players safely
home. Most of these boys went
overseas in the next year or so to
serve their country in World War I.

Barry Maxner

Learning to Play the Game

The ponds and outdoor rinks were the places to find Canadian children developing their hockey skills in the early 1900s, just the same as their forebears had done in the early 1800s when hockey was evolving. Any thought of an organized minor hockey program was yet to be developed and lay sometime in the distant future. Great hockey was played and great players were developed on those ponds, which gave rise to teams of all ages that made up the exciting district leagues.

Girls were often required by older boys to skate at one end of the pond, leaving most of the space for boys' games. However, a few feisty females overruled the would-be dominant males of the pond and got involved in the games. Of course, they were on their way to becoming members of one of the town's outstanding women's teams of the future.

Also, with the help of parents, children flooded, shovelled, and scraped the natural ice surfaces of outdoor rinks to ensure that they always had a place to skate and to play the good old hockey game.

As time went on, adult supervision and teaching developed and more and better youth teams appeared. By 1910, teams were organized into leagues and indoor games were being played whenever money could be raised to pay for rink ice time. Twelve players at 10 cents apiece paid the hourly ice rental of $1.20. Oh, the thrill of playing your first game inside the rink, out of the wind, and without having to use up all your energy scraping the ice before you could play. At $1.20 an hour, that service was provided by the management. Teams were sponsored by the Boy Scouts, the YMCA, and various churches and schools, and gave most everybody who wanted to play an opportunity to get involved. The high school had a team which competed with similar teams in adjacent towns and often got involved in a provincial play-off at the end of the season. Trophies were offered for the Junior League, often by the local newspaper, interested citizens, or community groups. The children who took part at this level had great fun while developing physical skills and learning lessons about teamwork and team spirit which would serve them throughout their lives, and not only in hockey. And when the high school team won the Nova Scotia Provincial High School Championship, as Windsor first did in 1919, it caused as much excitement in town as the Stanley Cup play-offs do these days! Junior hockey in those times served to fill long winter hours for restless youth, developed minds and bodies, shaped lives, and created memories to last a lifetime.

At the turn of the century, skates and boots each cost $2 a pair and had to be joined with small screws that came in the skate box from the Starr Manufacturing Company, along with a free catalogue of other skates and hockey sticks and an updated copy of the rules of ice hockey. Shin pads were homemade, and a hockey cost a quarter. Not counting sweater, pants, and socks, the total cost of an outfit was $4.25.

MORE EQUIPMENT, MORE MONEY *By 1914, more hockey equipment had been developed, and the cost of various items was as follows:*	
Boots	*2.00*
Skates	*2.00*
Toque	*0.35*
Jersey	*2.00*
Knickers	*1.00*
Gloves	*3.25*
Socks	*0.75*
Shinpads	*0.75*
Hockey Stick	*0.50*
Puck	*0.35*
Total	*$12.95*

Let There Be Ice and Ice Makers

It seemed as if everybody wanted to get into the game. Ice time was booked in the new covered rink from morning till evening, with just enough hours left over for the dedicated ice-making staff to prepare a new sheet overnight for the following day's activities. The ice makers had to know their stuff and use every opportunity during cold snaps to build up the thickness of the ice. It was necessary to have a little excess to come and go on during soft spells and at the end of the season, when temperatures made it nearly impossible to maintain a good skating surface. That usually came at the end of March, so the season, which seldom got underway much before December 25, was never more than three months long.

Sports Reports

After 1900, newspapers were beginning to report the outcome of important league games, and ads were beginning to appear announcing upcoming important games. Sports accounts appeared as minor items, mixed in with other news reports, on the front page, only if they warranted it, and were very brief except in special cases.

THE WINDSOR SWASTIKAS — Windsor's team won the Western Nova Scotia Senior title in 1910. The members are shown here sporting the Halifax *Herald* and *Mail* Trophy. The swastika was used by many cultures to signify "good fortune" before being appropriated to become the symbol of Hitler's infamous Third Reich.

Garwin Smith

The sports reporter's terminology, understood, accepted, and relished by the sports faithful today, was yet to be developed. The sport section in newspapers was far in the future.

Leagues, Legends, Fans, and Rivals

By 1910, hockey leagues were established for both males and females of most age groups and all walks of life. Hockey legends were beginning to be moulded in the Windsor Rink as elsewhere in the country, and most certainly the hockey fans of the town and surrounding area were well established. Team loyalties were becoming deepseated. Windsor and nearby Kentville were fast becoming fierce hockey rivals, as happened in neighbouring towns and cities in every province.

The Windsor Swastikas

Long before Adolph Hitler and the Third Reich began to use the swastika as a symbol for their organization in Nazi Germany, the emblem was used by a variety of cultures all over the world. It signified good fortune. Like the Greeks, Romans, and American Indians, one senior hockey team in Windsor adopted the swastika in 1910. Team members displayed the emblem on their hand-knit, turtleneck wool sweaters and became an outstanding hockey team with very good fortune indeed. The team was spearheaded by the high-scoring, fast-skating showman, Blaine Sexton. The Swastikas were the team to beat in their area. They went on an annual road trip, or hockey excursion, to Newfoundland, and played the best the island had to offer along the path of the famous "Newfie Bullet" train as they visited and played hockey from Port-aux-Basques to St. John's. One photo of the famous Swastikas, taken by a photographer in St. John's at the easterly end of the trip, shows the team in their white home-knit jerseys displaying the likewise handmade emblems. The Swastikas performed from 1910 until 1916, when most of the play-

SWASTIKAS HAD "HOME" AND "AWAY" OUTFITS AS EARLY AS 1910 — Between 1910 and 1916, the team made several trips to Newfoundland to take part in competitions along the way from Port-aux-Basques to St. John's.

Garwin Smith

WINDSOR'S YMCA HOCKEY TEAM, 1911 — The YMCA sponsored hockey teams throughout the Maritimes in the early 1900s. Windsor's team won the town league trophy.

Geraldine Marcotte

ers had gone overseas in World War I. Word has it that the Swastikas were loved wherever they went and were never beaten on "The Rock." This could be the reason the Swastikas returned to the island to play each year, but more likely it was because of the "Newfie hospitality," which "might be equalled, but never bettered, b'y!"

The 1920s and 1930s

By the 1920s, hockey leagues were buzzing in towns all across Canada. Professionalism was taking the very best players to the big league teams, but there were still plenty of excellent players in the small towns to more than satisfy the local fans with first-class amateur hockey. Most small towns had a couple of senior teams and teams for high school boys as well as school girls and young women. The hockey activity in Windsor was typical of that in most Canadian towns of the same size.

Amateurs Through and Through

Professionalism was slow to creep into Windsor, and when the town's senior team won the Provincial Senior Hockey Championship in 1922 and again in 1923, it did so with 100 per cent local talent.

Ice Hockey for Everybody

In Windsor, the town league had the Bankers, made up of accountants and bank clerks; the Firemen; the local farmers' team, called the Ramblers; a church team called the Four Squares; and the Eurekas, representing the local cotton mill.

United We Stand

A young men's social group called the Four Squares, sponsored by the Baptist Church, met weekly and was quite popular during the 1920s and 1930s. The Four Squares group in Windsor was socially significant for two important reasons: 1) the membership was not made up entirely of Baptists but represented several other churches as well (rather unusual for those times); and 2) this ecumenical group had an excellent hockey team which won the town league Citizens' Trophy seven years in a row. The town council presented the team with a special, large silver trophy in honour of the achievement in this highly competitive league.

The Valley Senior League

The official town team, called the Windsor Maple Leafs, represented the town in the Annapolis Valley Senior League. Barely a night went by in town without a game, as the rafters rang with shouts and cheers and the sound of the boards being pounded with fists and sticks when goals were scored or fights broke out (fun things one never does while watching hockey on TV!). The Windsor Rink had no seating space. You were either lucky enough to get a standing space along the four-foot-high boards surrounding the ice surface, or else you stood on the second- or third-row bleachers and looked over the heads of those more fortunate.

God help the short of limb at a hockey game in those days. The regulars always wanted to stand in their own special spot where they could lean over the ice surface, see all the action, and yell out important instructions to members of both teams.

Between Periods

"Hold my spot!" always preceded a flying trip to the front of the rink to Mr. Herb Smith's canteen for a hot dog and a Coke, between periods, of course. Military band music played over the loudspeakers helped to pass the time while the players went to the dressing rooms, mopped their brows, got their breath, and made their plans for the next period. Everybody knew the tunes on the speakers and many clapped time to the music in an attempt to warm chilled fingers, while others actually marched their feet up and down to stimulate the blood flow through their numb toes.

When the players finally glided back onto the ice to begin another period, fans forgot about their cold limbs and got back to the shouting and board banging.

Everybody on the Ice

The boards around the ice surface in the old Windsor rink were made in sections and not intended to hold back unlimited weights. Therefore it was no surprise, on occasion, for a section to give way when folks were leaning heavily to catch a glimpse of the action at the other end of the rink. The fans would spill onto the ice in a screaming heap, bringing the game to a sudden halt. The ice makers, Ned and Fred Carmichael, would have to come with hammers and spikes and put people and boards back in their places so the teams could get on with the game.

National Anthem Stops Fights

The management always kept a 78-rpm record of "God Save The King" next to the record player in Windsor to play loud and clear over the loudspeaker system whenever the referees had trouble breaking up a fight. Many of us remember a vicious fight that was broken up one night by playing the anthem: the players stood at attention until the last strains of the anthem finished, only then to start fighting again. The anthem began once more, and the players suddenly stood at attention. It had to be played three times before the players finished their fight.

Winning the Pool

Around town, the day following a town league match, the talk was all about "last night's game," and the leading question was, "Who won the pool on the game?" Some of the locals were forever selling tickets (10 cents apiece and three for a quarter) on a $5 or $10 pool on the score of the games. A ten-spot wasn't to be sneezed at in those years.

The Trip to the Game

In the early 1900s, before motorcars were widely used, Mr. Charlie Dill and others used to transport Windsor teams to Hantsport and Wolfville, seven and 18 miles away, by horse and sleigh.

Later, when automobiles became available and the town teams went to play in other Annapolis Valley towns, the players often travelled in the back of a truck stuffed with hay for insulation against winter's cold. At other times they would travel, six in a car, just like many of the fans who went to support them. Those big Valley Senior games were the most exciting things that happened in the lives of fans through the long winter months. Regardless of the weather or road conditions, they were there, week after week, players and fans, for their all important hockey games. It was a way of life then.

The "DAR Special"

For special games and at play-off time in the Annapolis Valley Senior League, the Dominion Atlantic Railway, referred to as the "DAR," always ran special hockey trains to carry large numbers of fans who wouldn't miss the play-offs. Those were very special small

DAR Hockey Special — The Flying Bluenose steamed into Windsor with fans from Kentville, and from whistle stops along the way, to attend hockey games in the old Windsor Rink. These "hockey trips" were made regularly in the early to mid-1900s.

Postcard, Valentine and Sons

AD FROM THE *ACADIAN RECORDER*, 1904.

town social events, peculiar to the era. The pattern, established in the early 1920s, continued for three decades, right through World War II. Ice hockey, trains, and hockey fans were inseparable in the Maritimes. The special hockey trains, put on for matches between Kentville and Windsor, served to carry a carload or two of exuberant fans from one town to the other. The fans were out not only to see the game but also to stir up a little fun and excitement on the side. And if a fight just happened to break out in the rink or at the railway station, well, they weren't above taking part in that either. So intense was the rivalry that fans filled the rinks to the rafters, and sometimes they filled the rafters as well. Talk about your rivalries! It went on between Kentville and Windsor for a full six decades.

Kentville, Nova Scotia, was the headquarters of the Dominion Atlantic Railway and a very proud hockey town. The Kentville Wildcats were just that — wild cats — as far as the colourful Windsor Maple Leafs were concerned. In all other seasons of the year, the players and fans were cordial, but in winter things changed and they became serious adversaries. On the evening of a match in Windsor, the Kentville fans would climb aboard the special DAR three-car train lined up at the station, headed for Windsor. This forms an important part of the hockey heritage of the Annapolis Valley. As the train made its way through the valley, it stopped for fans who would be anxiously awaiting its arrival in Wolfville, Grand Pré, Hantsport, and Falmouth, plus a few whistle stops along the way. They had to be ready, for she'd just slow down long enough for them to get aboard, then speed on toward the valley's oldest railway station and covered rink in Windsor.

A Party Along the Way

True, they were going to Windsor to see a hockey game, but they were having a party on the way. That was an important part of the trip. Most nights things stayed pretty well under control, some fans playing cards and others making music, but on certain occasions, especially at play-off time, the train cars sometimes ended up the worse for wear, as did some of the fans. Money and entertainment were both scarce, and it's no wonder that the train trips to the rinks were so popular. Most couldn't afford a car, but there weren't many who couldn't raise the price of a ticket on the DAR and a pint or a little apple cider. After all, this was the apple capital of the world and cider was very easy to come by, and it certainly made those cold winter evenings a lot happier.

TUESDAY, JAN. 12 - 8 P. M.

2 - HOCKEY GAMES - 2

PROVINCIAL LEAGUE:

WANDERERS VS. NEW GLASGOW.

INTERMEDIATE LEAGUE:

WANDERERS VS. D. Y. M. C. A.

ADMISSION 25 CENTS.　　　BALCONY 35 CENTS.

EMPIRE RINK. H.B.CLARKE, LESSEE & MANAGER.

Buses and Pick-up Trucks

The boards would be pretty well lined with Windsor fans when the train crossed the bridge over the Avon and trundled into the old station. Some of the Windsor fans came from down the shore as far as Walton, 30 miles away, on Doran's bus or in the back of a pick-up truck to witness the most exciting thing to happen in their lives since the last game. The rafters would ring and the boards would clatter as everybody leaned forward to get a good view of the action as the players flew by. With the arrival of the fans from the railway station, the crowd just packed in a little tighter and somehow made room for everybody.

The Donnybrook and the Aftermath

Fights between players were common and between fans not uncommon. The difference was that the players stopped fighting when the game was over, while the fans could continue all the way to the railway station and then some. Hockey sticks were sometimes used to break train windows on troublesome nights, and old fashioned fists were the cause of many a bruise and black eye.

Here Comes the Judge

Bill Taylor, at age 90, recalls one particular trip home from a game in Windsor, when a DAR conductor was mistaken for a cop by a friend of his who had been slightly over-served. The fan, who didn't think the "cop" should be on the train interfering with their party, took him down with one wild swing of his fist. Train officials took a list of those on board that night, and within days they all appeared at a special enquiry at the Kentville courthouse to account for their actions.

Memories for a Lifetime

The achievements of Windsor's hockey teams up to and including the World War II years mirror those of many Canadian towns, in that they had their share of wins, provided much enjoyment, and created a lot of memories for both players and fans. Most fans and players involved in hockey in Windsor in those days were not aware of the fact that the game had originated less than a mile from the rink, on Long Pond. Nor would it have made much difference if they had known. For the thing that was most important to them at that time is still the most important thing for fans and players here: simply that they're involved, in one way or another, in the world's fastest and most exciting game, ice hockey!

CHAPTER 11

Women in Hockey

Vive la Différence

Because of the differences in size and body build, it is difficult for women and men to play hockey together. Canadian women in the early 1890s seemed to sense this and headed out on their own to take a crack at the great game that had recently taken the nation by storm. In Nova Scotia, there weren't too many towns that didn't have

EDMONTON LADIES' HOCKEY TEAM, 1899 — The ladies apply their Starr Acme Club skates, which clamp directly to the soles and heels of their boots.   *PAA*

MARIE (SEXTON) PURNELL MUSSER —
Captain of the Ladies' Team at
Acadia in 1924, Marie recalls
playing pond hockey with her
brother, Blaine Sexton, who later
became England's outstanding
hockey star in the 1920s and 1930s.

Marie (Sexton) Purnell Musser

WOMEN TOOK THEIR ICE HOCKEY VERY
SERIOUSLY IN THE EARLY 1900s — At
the time, the game was just settling
in on the West Coast and covered
rinks were popping up all across the
country. Ice hockey was fast
becoming our great winter game
and the women of our nation were
having their piece of the action.

a team or two of young ladies eager for competition. It's not known for certain exactly when girls picked up hockeys, but to be sure, it wasn't long after the boys did. When reporters began recording their games in newspapers in the early 1900s, it was obvious that the brand of game they played was quite different from that played by men at the time. Reporters commenting on ladies' games in the *Acadian Recorder* used phrases such as "rosy cheeked" and "pretty girls" as opposed to "rough," "hard hitting," and "enemy" used to describe men's games.

Edmonton Ladies and Nova Scotia Skates

One of the earliest photos of women in hockey outfits is that of an Edmonton Ladies Team, taken in 1899 when the population of the town was a mere 2000, the same as that of Windsor, Nova Scotia, in the same year. The photo shows the women applying skates to their boots with the famous clamping method invented by John Forbes of the Starr Manufacturing Company of Dartmouth, Nova Scotia, in 1865. Photos of hockey teams were relatively new then, so this one gives a rare glimpse of the Nova Scotia-made skates as they were applied to the players' boots. These were exactly the same kind of skates used by the Montreal men's teams when they began to play Nova Scotia's ice game in 1875. At the time, Starr held the patent, so other companies had not yet begun to produce clamp-on skates. (The clamp-on model was cheap and remained popular into the 1930s, even though far more sophisticated models were available.)

THE ACADIA UNIVERSITY SEMINARY LADIES' HOCKEY TEAM, 1924 — They used Pirate hockey sticks, made in Wolfville, and competed with ladies' teams in adjacent Annapolis Valley towns.

Marie (Sexton) Purnell Musser

TIME OUT FOR A PHOTO — One snowy day in the winter of 1926, the Windsor Ladies' Hockey Team stepped outside the shingled rink for a photo opportunity with their coach and manager.

Katherine "Kay" Anslow

The Outfits They Wore

The most remarkable thing noted in early photos of women playing hockey is the fact that they all wore long heavy skirts which hung down almost to the ice surface. Such costumes must have impaired both speed and stickhandling ability immensely.

Their sticks were the same as those used by the men, and, of course, we know that they had little in the way of protective equipment, because it just had not been invented yet. Hands were covered with mittens or ordinary kid leather gloves. Gauntlets (as hockey gloves were first called) did not appear until after the turn of the century.

Turtleneck sweaters formed an important part of the ladies' outfit for decades, supplying the warmth and comfort needed in the natural ice rinks. Matching toques or stocking caps, often with tassels, completed the set.

AMHERST RAMBLERS LADIES' TEAM — The great amount of white tape on these ladies' hockey sticks suggests either that the players were nurses with access to hospital supplies, or that their sticks were due for replacement. The Starr skates, screwed to high-heeled boots, together with the long skirts and the absence of gloves dates the photo to the 1890s. The crests on their jerseys are the flying skates used by the first Maritime Senior Champions, the Amherst Ramblers of 1904.

Al Hartlen

Farewell to Long Skirts

As time went on, things got steadily rougher in women's hockey. The sore-shin problem developed and was soon solved by the invention of shinpads. At first, shinpads, made of strips of bamboo cane that

were placed under a layer of thin leather and stitched to harness felt, was all that was available. Like everybody else playing hockey, the ladies wanted these, not only to protect their shins from whacks with sticks but also for the status they afforded them. The faster, rougher hockey and the wearing of shinpads necessitated a change in uniform. The long heavy skirts were replaced with equally heavy woolen bloomers. The bloomers kept the body warm and at the same time allowed the new shinpads to be worn outside the wool stockings. Then, when kneepads became popular, short pants and long wool stockings with circular stripes became the usual garb for both males and females playing the game. The whole hockey outfit had changed completely in the course of a few short years.

Skates with Ankle Supports

The clamp-on skates on which hockey was played after 1865 were gradually replaced with newer versions as the Starr Manufacturing Company continued to supply hockeyists with the best product possible. Just as the much loved Starr hockey skate was developed for men, so the Ladies' Beaver skate was developed for women. The single steel blades were permanently attached to the boots in the factory. The boots were extra high so as to rise well above the ankles and provide better support and protection from injury. Also, a special ankle strap crossed from the inner to the outer side of the foot across the forefoot and was tightened with a metal buckle.

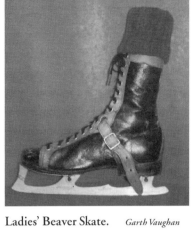

Ladies' Beaver Skate.　*Garth Vaughan*

IRISH WOMEN'S CAMOGIE (HURLEY) TEAM, 1904 — The women's version of hurley (the Irish field game from which hockey developed) is called "camogie."

Gaelic Athletic Association, Dublin

Road Trips and the Works

The Windsor Ladies' Hockey Team competed annually with the ladies' teams from nearby Hantsport, Wolfville, Acadia University, Middleton, and Stewiacke. Cooperative male hockey players coached the ladies, refereed their games, and accompanied them on road trips to adjacent towns. The ladies performed only exhibition games in this area, never competing for a trophy. Wonderful skaters, they seemed interested only in playing the game for the sport itself. To many in those times, hockey was still a game, and the ladies were content to get in some ice time a couple of times a week to push the puck around and improve their stickhandling skills. A trip out of town to test those skills against their counterparts in the Annapolis Valley was an exciting bonus. After the games, there was often a free skate and social time with the other team, and, if they were lucky, a lunch before they headed home.

In 1910, the Halifax Ladies' Hockey Team travelled to Windsor to play the magnificent Windsor Ladies' Team. Halifax put up a good struggle only to be trounced by a score of 18-0.

The girls showed the world that day that it wasn't only the Windsor men and boys who could walk off with top honours in hockey. The rover on the Windsor team at the time was Hazel Sexton, sister of Blaine Sexton (who became the outstanding hockey star of Europe in the 1920s and 1930s). Hazel was known for her sensational wrist shot and she scored no fewer than nine of the 18 goals that day. Hazel and Dot Mosher, sister of Nova Scotia hockey legend Ernie Mosher, sparked women's hockey in Windsor for a number of years. Following their hockey careers, they appeared regularly at the skating rink and were two of the smoothest skaters imaginable. They served as wonderful examples of the graceful art of skating for yet another generation of Windsor's skatists and hockeyists.

The Wet End of the Season

In addition to shortening the hockey season to a fleeting three months, natural ice cramped the style of hockeyists, both male and female, in other ways back in the 1920s. Warm spring days meant that many a play-off game was played on spongy and sometimes downright wet ice. A fall on the ice meant that kneepads, gloves, stockings, and sweaters all got soaked. But worst of all, according to the women, was the amount of water that was sopped up by the seat of those big, heavy blue wool bloomers. Oh, that artificial ice had been invented 20-30 years sooner!

WINDSOR LADIES' HOCKEY TEAM, 1924 — Mable Smith, Edna Norris, Babe Caldwell, Nano Ward, Aletha Card, Essie Mounce, Dot Mosher. Very high boots with ankle-support straps were worn by all members of this team, who also used the same hairstyle. The buns of hair were known as "cooty garages," an in-house joke with the girls. "Cooty" was a slang expression for head lice, and the "garages," of course, were home! Notice that the team mascot, Jean Reid, is wearing double-blade bob skates, used by beginners.

Bill Giles

CHAPTER 12

The Coloured Hockey League
of the Maritimes

At the turn of the century, ice hockey fever struck Canada and everybody seemed to be catching it. Leagues were being formed all across the nation. It seemed as if every school, college, church, bank, and business had a hockey team and hoped for a championship and the possession of a trophy as well as a year-end photo of the team with the trophy in the local paper to prove it.

Conditions Same for Most Canadians

Conditions had become much the same for most players no matter where they were playing in the country, but not so for the Blacks and the Natives. Many towns didn't have either, of course, but in towns where they did live, it was difficult for them to break into the

JOHN PARIS SR. AND THE CURRY'S CORNER BULLDOGS, 1939 — Back row: John Paris Sr., Ken Hergett, Ellis Seary, Don Dill, Oren Rourke, Fred Palmer, Henry Sanford, Halton Rourke. Front row: Bill Isenberg, Bruce Morison, Lawrence Hergett, Stan Hergett, Jack Morison, Harold "Hip" Brown. The Bulldogs played in the Windsor Town League before World War II. The one Black member of the team was an outstanding baseball player as well. John "Buster" Paris Sr. returned from overseas to play hockey and baseball in the town league. One son, Percy, played hockey for King's College School, and another son, John Jr., advanced to Junior A hockey in Quebec and, in 1994, became the first Black head coach in professional hockey.

Lillian Hergett

JOHN PARIS JR. OF WINDSOR —
In May 1994, John Paris Jr. of
Windsor, as the first Black head
coach in professional hockey, led
the Atlanta Knights to the IHL
Championship. After playing great
hockey in his home town, John was
scouted by Scotty Bowman and then
played Junior A hockey in Quebec
before becoming a scout for the St.
Louis Blues from 1987 to 1991.
Prior to joining Atlanta, John was
coach and general manager of the
St. Jean Lynx team in the Quebec
Major-Junior Hockey League,
where he had coached for two
decades. John Jr. gives credit to his
father, John Paris Sr., for his early
achievements in both hockey and
baseball and is proud to be
coaching the Knights, the chief farm
team of the Tampa Bay Lightning.

Knightline Magazine

mainstream. Some got to play but most did not. Generally they were not well accepted. There are lots of stories of prejudice preventing them from playing hockey over many years. On the reserves, the Natives formed teams and played the game by themselves, usually on ponds and outdoor rinks. It was the same with the Blacks.

The Black community in the Maritimes, seeking to be a part of the great new wave of winter sporting activity as well as attempting to overcome their position of repression, formed teams in several communities and engaged in exhibition games in the late 1890s. By 1900, they had formed the Coloured Hockey League of the Maritimes, quite likely the only such hockey league in the world. And at the end of each season, when the championship was awarded, it was also likely the Coloured Hockey Championship of the World as well as of the Maritimes.

The first Black community in Nova Scotia, direct from Africa, dates back to 1741. Also in the 1700s, Black United Empire Loyalists, 2000 in number, settled in the province, and in 1812 another 2000 arrived from the United States.

Black athletes in Nova Scotia have been making a strong statement in sports for a long time, and ice hockey was one of the first games in which they excelled. By 1900, a league had been formed with teams in Africville, Dartmouth, Halifax, Truro, and Amherst. Prince Edward Island had one Black team, which played exhibition games with the famous all-white team on the Island, the Abegweits of Charlottetown, and with the Black teams of Nova Scotia. The Halifax city team was called the Eurekas and the Dartmouth team was known as the Jubilees. The team representing the community of Africville was known as the Seasides, and Hammonds Plains was represented in the league by the Moss Backs. The Truro team operated under the name of the Victorias and nearby Amherst called its team the Royals.

You Are Cordially Invited

Games between city and out-of-town teams were arranged by formal invitation, and some of these are recorded in the newspapers of the day. Following the games, the visiting team was entertained by the host team. In Halifax, the Eureka Hall on Maynard Street was the usual site of such meetings, where a dinner and get-together were enjoyed by the team members. Across the harbour in Dartmouth, post-game celebrations were usually held at the Queen Hotel. Cordial letters of appreciation were sent to the host team along with an invitation for a return match.

Good Hockey, Plus

The style of ice hockey played by these teams was both exciting and
entertaining and was described by reporters as rough, tough, and
acrobatic. The Coloured Hockey League provided great entertainment for large audiences of predominantly white fans. Between
periods, the players entertained with special skating and displays of
circus-like comedy. The fans expected acrobatical, flamboyant, out-
of-the-ordinary hockey with plenty of mix-ups, body checks and
high-jumping exhibitions. And they got it! At a time when 300-400
attendance was a good crowd in the Halifax Rink, these teams were
drawing as many as 1200 a game.

> *Players for the Amherst Royals in
> 1904 were: Martin, Cummings, H.
> Ross, G. Ross, Lee, Parsons, and
> Cook.*

The Empire and the New Exhibition Rinks

Games in Halifax were played in the Empire Rink and the New Exhibition Rink. The regular admission for senior games was 25 cents,
and balcony seats were 35 cents. Two-column announcements in the
Halifax newspapers were paid for by the rink management as an in-
vestment, because large crowds meant good profits, and attendance
was excellent at most games, due to the popularity of hockey in general and the Coloured League in particular.

> Hockey,
> The Eurekas and Royals of Amherst,
> play at the North End Rink Saturday
> night. The West End Rangers leave
> Charlottetown next Monday, play at Truro
> Thursday and at the North End Rink 20
> and 21.

NOTICE OF BLACK HOCKEY GAMES
IN THE *ACADIAN RECORDER*,
FEBRUARY 11, 1903

AD FROM THE *ACADIAN RECORDER* - 1904.

In 1904, the line-up for the Eurekas was as follows:

Goal	Allison
Point	Flint
Cover Point	Taylor
L. Wing	Toliver
R. Wing	Skinner
Centre	Adams
Rover	Adams

A Ten-Year Treasure

The league operated regularly from 1900 to 1910, at which point activity declined somewhat. Exhibition games continued into the 1920s on a more or less regular basis and sporadically after that. The *Canadian Hockey Year Book* of 1923 noted that a number of games were played between Black teams in Nova Scotia during the year but that no regular championship was decided.

The Days of the Rover

Games in the 1900-1910 period were played with seven players a side, including the rover, which was the custom all across Canada at the time. All players were on the ice for the entire game and played two half-hour periods with a ten-minute break at half-time. Delays of 10 or 15 minutes were not uncommon during a game while a player recovered from an injury enough to continue the game or while a broken skate was repaired. Since each team consisted of seven players who played the entire game, if a player was unable to complete the game because of injury, the other team reduced its number by one and the game went on with six a side. This was to satisfy a no-replacement rule that was in effect in the league at that time.

Black Goalies First to Go to Ice

The Coloured League made a contribution to ice hockey that has had far-reaching effects on the game. The league method of play differed in one respect from others in the country: the goaltender was allowed to get down on the ice to stop the puck. In all other leagues in the country the goalkeeper was required to stand for the entire game and was penalized for going down. Goaltenders elsewhere were not allowed down on the ice until the season of 1917-18.

Shinpads, without knee protection, were the only protective equipment used. Single-blade skates, screwed onto boots, were the common type, as tube skates were new on the market, relatively expensive, and not yet popular. Gauntlets, or hockey gloves, were just beginning to appear. Most players used ordinary work gloves and many played in bare hands.

Road Trip to Cape Breton

In March of 1904, the Halifax Eurekas and the Dartmouth Jubilees travelled to Cape Breton for exhibition games. The *Acadian Recorder* of Halifax, in announcing the forthcoming "first games of hockey played in Cape Breton by coloured people," assured the fans that they could "expect good sport." A game was played in North Sydney on a Monday night, followed by games in Sydney on Tuesday and Wednesday. The games were well attended and caused great excitement at both rinks.

Interprovincial Play

The West End Rangers of PEI visited the mainland to play teams in the Halifax rinks, travelling by ferry and train, as there were no motor cars available at the time. The Mills family of Summerside made up five of the seven players on the Rangers team and played havoc with the team when two of them left the island to move to New Glasgow. The other two players for the Rangers were McNeil and Ryan.

Local prejudices were sometimes reflected in the reports of games appearing in newspapers, and players were not always treated with the respect they deserved in some of the rinks where they played. Generally poor, the players struggled to acquire the basic equipment, organize teams, and raise money to pay for ice time. There is no evidence that a trophy of any kind ever existed to denote supremacy in the league, even though the Black community actively competed for a championship in the Maritimes for a full decade.

AD FROM THE *ACADIAN RECORDER*, 1904.

AD FROM THE *ACADIAN RECORDER*, 1904.

CHAPTER 13

Local Hockey Legends

Some Stand Out Above the Rest

Along with the development of the game and its equipment, there appeared outstanding players and teams. All worked to perform at their best level of achievement in a game that became faster, rougher, and more complicated with each successive season. Obsessed with the game and willing to apply themselves to the fullest, many achieved a high level of skill. There were always a few on each team who stood out above the rest, as is the case to this day. In each and every town some players were so good and provided such enjoyment for the fans that they became hockey legends in their own time. Like all hockey towns, Windsor has its share of legends. They developed as soon as leagues were formed and town battled town for hockey supremacy. Prior to 1900, records of games were sparse and incomplete. The players who learned the game and carried it to others prior to the 1880s must, for now, remain nameless legends. Turn-of-the-century stories of greatness passed from generation to generation

WINDSOR HOCKEY CHAMPIONS OF 1889 — One of Canada's oldest hockey team photos shows the players wearing medallions, won in previous years, before trophies became available. They are also displaying handmade hockey sticks. Phillip Hamilton, a team member and wheelwright by trade, wrote in his diary that he "roughed out hockey sticks" and, later, that he "completed hockey sticks." Note the blade shape and rounded handles. The Windsor Juniors was one of several teams competing for top honours in town in 1889. The Blue Jackets, Alerts, and Avonians lost out to the Juniors for the town championship. The Juniors also played matches with Acadia University, King's College, Hantsport, and the Halifax Athletes. The team played its games on Flat Iron Pond, in the centre of town, the present site of Victoria Park. Back row: John Powers, George Smith, Herbert Silver, Alonzo Sweet, William McInnis. Middle row: James Forsyth, Richard Flemming, Percy Curry, Allison Smith. Front row: Alex McInnis, Phillip Hamilton.

WHHC

among the hockey faithful. One Windsor player of that era, Phillip Hamilton, was mentioned in write-ups of town hockey and football, and he was so interested that he kept a diary that gives us a glimpse of the life of a legend in those early times in the 1880s. After 1900, newspaper reporters began recording their impressions of the calibre of play of both teams and individuals and made it easy for us to know about the great achievers, the favourites of the fans.

WINDSOR ACADEMY HOCKEY TEAM, 1919 — Back row: John "Chook" MacDonald, Jim Reid, H. Carleton Smith. Front Row: John MacDonald, Sammy Macdonald, Tommy Winning, Ernie Mosher. These seven wonders could trim both the local senior team and the Acadia University team and took the provincial high school championship with ease. "Cy" Smith went on to play for King's and Dalhousie universities, Sammy MacDonald played for Boston, and Ernie Mosher led the Halifax Wolverines to the Allan Cup championship. They are all wearing single-blade skates. The goalie stick (wide-on-one-side) was the first wide-type stick to be used in Nova Scotia.

WHHC

NOVA SCOTIA SENIOR CHAMPIONS, 1923 — The Windsor Hockey Club won the Provincial Senior Title in two consecutive years (1922 and 1923) with 100 per cent local talent. Back row: W. A. Ryan, F. Clark, E. Mosher, G. McElhiney. Middle row: V. McCann, G. Smith, J. Hughes. Front row: S. MacDonald, F. Poole, C. McDonald, R. Cochrane.

Aubrey McCann

ERNIE MOSHER: THE WINDSOR WIZARD — Newsmen dubbed Ernie Mosher the Windsor Wizard, and they said he was the best hockey player in Nova Scotia in the 1920s. He led his high school team to the provincial championship in 1919 and did the same for the Windsor senior team in 1922 and 1923. He then joined the Kentville Wildcats, who captured the Maritime senior title. In 1935, he led the Halifax Wolverines to Nova Scotia's only Allan Cup championship.

Howard Dill

Hockey Families

Many towns can boast about the hockey achievements of certain families. The NHL has been blessed with such notables as the Patrick, Conacher, Bentley, Metz, Howe, and Mahovlich families.

Windsor is noted for hockey families also, including brother-sister achievers. Blaine Sexton achieved international recognition as a hockeyist in England and Europe, and three sisters, Marie, Josephine, and Hazel, all played good hockey in the early 1900s. Hazel was an outstanding high scorer with a wicked wrist shot in the days of the rover. Ernie Mosher, referred to as the greatest all-time

"Doggie" Kuhn — Mr. and Mrs. Fred Kuhn of Windsor brought up a family of hockey players. Mrs. Kuhn often said that, as a young boy, her son Gordon "Doggie" Kuhn put on his skates first thing in the morning and took them off when he went to bed. She said he skated on the road, to the pond and back, and wore his skates to the dinner table as well! His obsession with ice hockey paid off, for he made it to the NHL. He first played for Windsor junior and senior teams before he joined the Truro Bearcats and later the New Haven Eagles of the American Hockey League. "Doggie" got the nod from the NHL's New York Americans in the 1932-33 season.

Marjorie Baird

Blaine Sexton: Europe's "Mr. Hockey" — An outstanding, speedy, high-scoring member of the Windsor Swastikas, Blaine Sexton left the team and went overseas with the Canadian Army in World War I. A noted horseman, runner, football player, and all-round athlete, Sexton took his hockey gear with him when he went to war. He is credited by British sports writers of the era with having introduced organized hockey to England and therefore to Europe. While hockey had been played in a rudimentary form in England prior to that time, Sexton helped form a hockey team in the city of London called the London Lions, and he accelerated the formation of other competitive teams in Britain which led to formal competition within a league. The Lions remained the team to beat, and Sexton was Mr. Hockey in Europe for three decades. The fastest skater in the league as well as the highest scorer, he caused hockey excitement in Britain and on the continent during his entire hockey career. In 1924, Sexton played ice hockey with England during the Olympics. Blaine Sexton's unusual laminated rubber puck, used during his childhood, along with his Olympic jacket crest and photos of the famous London Lions are on display at the Windsor Hockey Heritage Centre.

Marie (Sexton) Purnell Musser

player in Nova Scotia, had siblings who also played well. His sister, Dot Mosher, was as smooth at stickhandling and scoring as she was on the blades. The Kuhn family brothers, Gordon "Doggie," Clarence "Skeet," and Harold, provided the Maritimes with much enjoyment in the rinks for a full decade. They starred on Windsor teams, and then "Skeet" Kuhn was outstanding as a goalie and "Doggie" Kuhn a great forward with Truro and Halifax teams as well. "Doggie" was one of the first Nova Scotians to make it to the American Hockey League and the NHL.

CHARLES "LONG-SHOT" CURRY — Charles Curry was called "Long-Shot," and many didn't know his first name. He was a tall, powerful pillar of the Windsor team in the early 1900s and was known for his quick and accurate puck-shooting ability. This special talent made him particularly popular with fans and idol of the youth of the area. Long-Shot was able to scoop the puck from his own end of the rink up and over the crossbeams, above the suspended electric lights, and land it in the net at the other end of the rink. How often he did that during regulation play is not known, but certainly often enough to earn his reputation and nickname.

WHHC

LEW SHAW, ROVER — In the early 1900s, the seventh player on the team was known as the rover. The position of rover was a creation of Nova Scotia, as were Mic-Mac sticks, Starr skates, goal nets, and rules of the game. The flashiest player on the team, the rover played where and how he wished. A fast, aggressive, high-scoring puck-hog who came through whenever he was required to do so, Lew Shaw filled the bill as an outstanding rover for Windsor in those times. A member of Nova Scotia's Sport Hall of Fame, Lew Shaw thrilled his own generation of Windsorians with his brilliant stickhandling. He was just as thrilling to the next generation, who gathered in his pool room in the centre of town to enjoy his Windsor hockey team photos and to listen to his wonderful hockey stories.

WHHS

FRANK POOLE — Frank Poole scored winning goals and pleased crowds in Windsor from high school to the Senior provincial championships. He was the kind of player who knew the game well and always came through when the team really needed him. His love of the game led him to become a favourite referee for many years in the Annapolis Valley following his brilliant hockey career.

Danny Dill

VIC MCCANN — Vic McCann started his hockey career when the point and cover point positions formed the back line. He became an outstanding defenceman during the time that Windsor captured Senior provincial titles in the 1920s. Following his retirement from hockey, he became a shopkeeper and displayed some of Windsor's hockey trophies and photos in his shop. He also spent time during the evenings telling his young fans stories of ice hockey in a previous era.

Danny Dill

BILL SINGER — The Collishaw Cup, donated by Ellis Collishaw, a wealthy Newfoundland businessman who loved Windsor's style of hockey, was the symbol of excellence combined with good sportsmanship in the Windsor town league in the early years. The cup, awarded according to popular vote by the fans, was often won by Bill Singer, a flashy young vet just back from World War I. Bill, who played on championship teams from early childhood, maintained his interest in the game throughout his life and became a respected referee in the Annapolis Valley area.

Danny Dill

LONDON LIONS ON TOUR IN EUROPE, 1920S — Blane Sexton (standing with cigarette) used single blade skates rather than tube skates his entire career.

Jim Wilcox

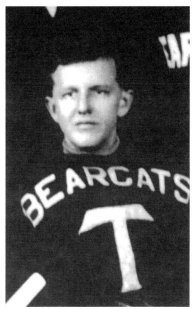

"Skeet" Kuhn — Clarence "Skeet" Kuhn developed his goaltending skills stopping puck shots made by some of the best hockey players in the province and first showed off his talents at all levels at home in Windsor. Later he played for the Truro Bearcats and Halifax Senior teams, particularly the famous Halifax Wolverines, in the early 1930s.

Howard Dill

Kay Anslow, the Editor of *The Hants Journal*, was also a hockeyist — Kay Anslow was a forward with the 1929 Windsor Ladies' Team. She is shown here sporting the new over-the-stocking kneepads that led to a change in women's costumes from ankle-length skirts to serge bloomers. Note her high-boot skates with buckled ankle supports, as well as her soft kid leather gloves, one-piece hockey stick, and single-blade skates. A well-respected all-round athlete, Kay pitched softball, golfed, curled, and played tennis as well as ice hockey.

Katherine "Kay" Anslow

SAMMY MACDONALD —
A member of the Windsor Senior
team that won the Nova Scotia
Senior Hockey Championship in
1922 and again in 1923, Sammy
MacDonald was an outstanding
defenceman and stickhandler. An
end-to-end rush artist, he went on
to play for Dartmouth, Halifax,
and the Boston Maples.

Walter MacDonald

HAZEL (SEXTON) WILCOX — Shown here at age 81, Hazel still had a good
wrist shot, which she developed as a child with her brother, Blaine Sexton.
He later became England's outstanding hockeyist in the 1920s and 1930s.
Hazel was the rover on the Windsor Women's Hockey Team in the early
1900s, and she continued to skate and have shots with her family well into
her eighties.

Helen Wilcox

REFEREES' WHISTLES — The "Dilly" whistle on the left was used by Windsor hockey legend Frank Poole, who was also a long-time referee in the Annapolis Valley in the 1920s and 1930s. The two-finger whistle was used by Walter Stephens, who served the Windsor area in the 1930s and 1940s.

Garth Vaughan

" B.N." BLAINE SEXTON, "THE FAMOUS INTERNATIONAL" — Sexton, ahead of his time as a hockeyist, took his hockey gear with him when he left Windsor and went to war. He became Europe's "Mr. Hockey" in the 1920s and 1930s. Captain of England's famous London Lions, he was once Speed Skating Champion of Europe and played for England in the 1924 Olympics.

Marie (Sexton) Purnell Musser

DOROTHY "DOT" MOSHER — A sister of the Windsor Wizard, Ernie Mosher, Dot could hold her own with any team. One of the smoothest skatists in Nova Scotia, she was a high-scoring forward for the Windsor Ladies Team in the mid-1920s.

Hilda Dill

Windsor hockey team, on tour —
Left to right: Frank Pool, Vic
McCann, Sam MacDonald, Bert
Ryan, Lloyd Taylor, Doggie Kuhn.
Shown in Charlottetown to play the
famous PEI "Abbies" in 1922.

Walter MacDonald

Chronology

1788 Founding of Canada's first college, King's College, at Windsor, Nova Scotia.

1796 Thomas Chandler Haliburton born in Windsor — lawyer, politician, judge, writer, who told of hurley being played on ice on Long Pond in Windsor, c. 1800.

1800-1900:
The Century of Development

c.1800 Hurley-on-ice, played in Windsor, Nova Scotia, on Long Pond, by students at King's College School.
Earliest reference to hurley being played on ice in Canada.
(Hurley-on-ice developed into ice hockey in Nova Scotia.)

1816 "The Devil's Punch Bowl and Long Pond, back of the College, were favourite resorts, and we used to skate in winter, on moonlight nights, on the ponds." (Windsor *Mail*)

1816 John Cunard of Halifax (brother of Sir Samuel Cunard of steamship fame), student at King's (1816-1819), has front teeth knocked out by Pete Delancey of Annapolis, N.S. while playing hurley on Long Pond. (From "Early Sketches of Windsor," *Windsor Mail*, 1876)

1829 "Every idler who feels disposed to profane the Lord's day may now . . . turn out with skates on feet, hurley in hand and play the delectable game of break-shins [hurley] without regard for the law." (Pictou *Colonial Patriot*)

1831 Hurley played on ice in Dartmouth by Irish workmen. Hurley is an Irish field game, and Irish immigrants in Dartmouth were building the Shubenacadie Canal, used by the Starr Manufacturing Company as a source of hydro power.

1831	"Excellent skating upon the head of the North West Arm, and large parties of our townsfolk and military, have enjoyed, during several afternoons of this and the past week, the healthy and spirit stirring game of wicket [hurley]." (Halifax *Nova Scotian*, Feb. 24, 1831)
1833	T.C. Haliburton buys land for his new residence, Clifton, including Long Pond, described in the deed as a "favourite skating place." (Long Pond is visible from Clifton and vice versa.)
1833	Miners play hurley on East River, Pictou. (Pictou *Colonial Patriot*, July 30, 1833)
1836	"In the winter when the ground is covered with snow, what grand times they have a-sleighin' over these here marshes with the gals, or playin' ball on the ice [hurley], or goin' to quiltin' frolics of nice long winter evenings, and then a-drivin' home like mad by moonlight." (T.C. Haliburton, *The Clockmaker*)
1838 to 1843	"In winter the common and almost only game was then called hurley, but now known as hockey. It was played either on foot on land, or on skates on ice." (Dalhousie *Gazette*, Dec. 2, 1887)
1842	"The Dartmouth Lakes . . . a game of ricket [hurley] . . . there is to be a great match today, if the weather be fine — which is very doubtful." (Halifax *Morning Post*, January 18, 1842)
1840s	The "Three Elms Cricket Club [of King's College, Windsor] . . . one of the events of the year for Windsor was the Encaenia Cricket Match . . . played with a team from the Halifax Garrison, who sometimes brought their band with them." (Cricket influenced the evolution of ice hockey.) (Hants *Journal*, Jan. 1970)
1844	*The Attaché,* by T.C. Haliburton, told of "hurley on the long pond on the ice."
1850	James George Aylwin Creighton born in Halifax — a pioneer of organized hockey in Canada.
1800 to 1850s	Ice hockey evolves from hurley-on-ice in Windsor-Halifax Dartmouth-Pictou area. Ice hockey has become a distinctive game with rules, the Halifax Rules.
1853	Hurley called a "Sabbath desecration." (Halifax *Acadian Recorder*, January 22, 1853)
1859	"Skates strapped on, and hurley in hand, the ball is followed over the glassy surface of the lakes, which ring to the skaters' heel." (Halifax *British Colonist,* Jan. 4,1859)

1859   Boston *Evening Gazette* sent to Halifax for sticks to intro-
        duce Nova Scotia's game to Boston. Ricket, wicket, hurley,
        and hockey were interchangeable terms in Nova Scotia.
        (Boston *Evening Gazette*, Nov. 15,1859)

1859   Terms hurley and hockey used interchangeably around
        Halifax. (C. Bruce Fergusson, N.S. provincial archivist,
        1965)

1860s   Mi'kmaq play hockey on Dartmouth Lakes with garrison
        troops. (Colonel Byron Weston, quoted by James Power,
        dean of Canadian sports writers, Halifax *Herald*, March 26,
        1943)

1860s   Wooden pucks used in hockey in Nova Scotia. (Colonel By-
        ron Weston)

1860   Prince of Wales (later King Edward VII) visited Windsor on
        Canadian and American tour.

1860s   Military travelling from Windsor and Halifax to England.

1863   Royal family play hockey on pond at Buckingham Palace.
        "Ten months after her marriage, the Princess of Wales rose
        abruptly from watching her husband play ice hockey and
        rushed home and delivered a son." (Robert K. Maffey, *The
        Dreadnaught)*

1860s   Rocks, called rickets, used to mark goal mouth in ice hockey.
        (Byron Weston)

1862   Halifax Skating Rink built, an indoor, covered rink (no
        hockey allowed).

1862   Victoria Skating Rink built in Montreal, an indoor, covered
        rink (hockey is 13 years away).

1864   "Halifax boys are playing hockey on the ice and occasion-
        ally mimicking the mistakes of such among their betters as
        are not quite at home on skates." (Halifax *Reporter*, January
        2, 1864)

1864   "Hockey ought to be sternly forbidden, as it is not only an-
        noying but dangerous." (Halifax *Morning Sun*, January 25,
        1864)

1865   T. C. Haliburton dies ten years before ice hockey spread to
        Montreal.

1865   Starr Manufacturing Company of Dartmouth produces
        Acme Club spring skates. Revolutionizes skating and hockey.
        Patented in 1866.

1865   Boys using Starr Acme skates play hurley on Lilly Lake,
        Saint John, New Brunswick. Many boys from Saint John
        attended King's College School in Windsor.

1867   Ricket and hockey played with hurleys on Dartmouth lakes by army and navy officers.

1867   British sailors and garrison officers play ice hockey at Halifax, on North West Arm.

1870   Windsor's first covered rink built at Fort Edward.

1870   William Henry Barker, a machinist of Windsor, patents a new skate.

1873   J.G.A.Creighton of Halifax moves to Montreal and introduces hockey to Montreal, becoming the "Father of Organized Hockey."

1873   In Halifax, hockey games last one hour, with a 10-minute break at half-time.

1875   First public game of ice hockey in Montreal, in Victoria Skating Rink, between teams from the Montreal Football Club and the Victoria Skating Rink.
       First game of hockey played inside a covered rink.

1876   Acadian boys play hockey at Bathurst, N.B.

1876   Stellarton Rink built.

1877   Metropolitan Men's Club of Montreal (J.G.A. Creighton, Secretary) rewrites rules of hockey using Halifax Hockey Club Rules and English Field Hockey Rules as guides.

1877   McGill University forms its first hockey club.

1878   Quebec City forms its first hockey team, which plays Montreal three years later.
       Hockey began to be played in three 30-minute periods.

1881   Quebec vs. Montreal.

1883   Hockey permitted to be played in a covered rink in Halifax for the first time, at Sarre's Rink, following a winter carnival (eight years after it was allowed to be played inside at Montreal).

1884   Cadet Roddy McColl, of New Glasgow, N.S., credited with teaching hockey to cadets at RMC in Kingston, Ontario. Actual game with Queen's two years away (1886).

1885   Dartmouth Rink (covered) built, and hockey played inside with seven men per team.

1886   Captains choose referee.

1886   New code of rules adopted by Amateur Hockey Association of Canada.

1886   RMC and Queen's University play first ice hockey game in Kingston with sticks from Nova Scotia.

1886   Admission price to hockey game in Halifax: 10 cents.

1887   Toronto telegraphs to Montreal for 18 sticks, pucks, and a set of rules to introduce hockey to Toronto.

1888   First organized hockey league in Nova Scotia.

1888   King's College of Windsor plays Dartmouth Ramblers on Dartmouth Lake.

1888   Windsor team beats King's 2-0 in Windsor Skating Rink at Fort Edward.

1888   Windsor Juniors play Dartmouth Athletes and win. Juniors also play Acadia University, Hantsport, and Horton Academy.

1888   Four hockey teams in Windsor: King's College, Alerts, Juniors, and Blue Jackets.
Four hockey teams in Dartmouth: Chebuctos Club (senior and junior), Ramblers, and Athletes.
Five hockey teams in Halifax: Crescents, Wanderers, North West Arm, Mutuals, and Dalhousie University.

1888   Dalhousie University and Dartmouth Chebuctos play a hockey game.

1888   In Ottawa, J.G.A. Creighton and the Stanley boys form the Rideau Hall Rebels Hockey Team.

1889   Kingston, Ontario, the Limestone City, forms its first hockey team.

1889   Forward passing introduced to Montreal by Dartmouth Chebuctos.

1890   Windsor plays four-game series with Dartmouth Chebuctos.

1890   Ontario Hockey Association formed.

1890   Winnipeg, Manitoba, forms its first hockey club, the Victorias.

1890   Victoria, B.C., forms its first hockey club.

1890s Regina and Calgary form hockey clubs.

1893   Winnipeg Victorias initiate the new face-off in ice hockey.

1893   Lord Stanley donates trophy (rose bowl) for senior amateur hockey championship of Canada.

1895   Lord Stanley and sons play ice hockey with royal dukes at Buckingham Palace (including the Prince of Wales, who became King Edward VII, and the Duke of York, who became King George V).

1893   Yale and Johns Hopkins universities begin playing ice hockey. (Boston knew of the game since 1859.)

1894   Philip Hamilton, Windsor hockey player, carves sticks for his team-mates, the Windsor Juniors.

1897   Starr Trophy presented by Starr Manufacturing Company for Halifax Hockey League, later used in Maritime Senior League (1904).

1899   Nova Scotia box net first used in Halifax game, Crescents vs. Wanderers, Jan. 6, 1899.
Nets used in Montreal on Dec. 30, 1899, at Westmount Rink, Shamrocks vs. Victorias.

1899   Canadian Amateur Hockey League formed.

1899   Admission to game in Halifax is 20 cents.

Significant Events after 1900: Ice Hockey's Second Century

1900   Nova Scotia box net accepted in Toronto.

1900   Coloured Hockey League formed in Maritimes. Goalkeeper allowed down on ice.

1902   Cost to attend game is 25 cents.

1902   Teams choose colours.

1904   International Hockey League formed.

1905   Dawson City Nuggets challenge Ottawa's Silver Seven for Stanley Cup. They travel 6000 miles in 23 days, at a cost of $3,000, and lose.

1908   Professionalism creeps (storms) into ice hockey. Accepted after 10 years of battles and team suspensions.

1908   National Hockey Association formed. Replaced with NHL in 1917.

1908   Stanley Cup used for Professional Championship of Canada.

1909   Sir Montague Allan, CVO, a prominent Montreal citizen, offers the Allan Cup for Amateur Senior Canadian Hockey Championship to replace the Stanley Cup.

1910   Top player fee is $3,000 (paid to both Lester and Frank Patrick by Renfrew Millionaires).

1911   Pacific Coast Hockey Association formed. First to play on artificial ice.

1911   Victoria Arena and Vancouver's Denman Arena, both with artificial ice plants, built by Frank and Lester Patrick.

1912   First artificial ice rink in Toronto, at the Arena Gardens, Dec.14, 1912.

1913   Rover position eliminated. Six players per team established.

1913   Referees first paid.

1914   Canadian Amateur Hockey Association formed.

1914   Allan Cup converted from challenge format to regional playdown system.

1917　NHL formed with four teams.

1917　NHL goalies allowed down on ice.

1917　Seattle Millionaires are the first American team to win the Stanley Cup.

1918　Professional players paid $450-$900 per season.

1919　Memorial Trophy donated by Captain James Sutherland of Kingston, Ontario, as a war memorial, for Canadian Junior Amateur Hockey Championship.

1920　Ice hockey first played at Olympics.

1931　Maple Leaf Gardens built — it houses 13 miles of pipes.

1933　Foster Hewitt begins broadcasting NHL games, establishing *Hockey Night in Canada*.

Glossary

Alchamadijik	Mi'kmaq term for hurley-on-ice.
Bandy	English game played with skates, sticks, and ball on ice.
Blacksmith	Craftsman who shapes iron to form implements, horseshoes, skates, etc.
Boards	In the game of ice hockey, the fence of wood about the ice surface that separates fans from the playing area.
Box Net	Name given to the first goal nets, which were devised and used in Halifax in 1899.
Bob Skates	Small-size, double-blade, sledlike skates used as learning device for small children.
Bully	In ice hockey, the term used to describe the release of the ball or puck to begin a game. It was replaced in Winnipeg in 1893 by the term "face-off."
Felts	Strips of blue felt 2" x $^1/_2$" x 12", that hockey players placed beneath skate laces, enabling them to tighten the fit of skates to their feet. Felts extruded like tongues over the toes of skate boots.
Gas Lamp	A lamp that burned coal gas, used to light the first indoor rinks from 1860s until 1890s when electric lights were invented.
Gauntlets	Name given to gloves with wrist protectors, first used in ice hockey in 1902, but not used by many players until some years later.
Goal Umpire	The judge of goals in early years of ice hockey. Stood on goal-line and rang a hand-bell to signify goals.
Hockeyist	One who plays ice hockey. A Canadian term, largely replaced with "hockey player" in 1920s.
Hockey	An English family name. A name used to describe the stick used in ice hockey. In the early years, hockey sticks were simply "hockeys."
Hurley (Hurling)	Irish field game played with sticks (hurleys) and ball (sliotar). When adapted to ice in Nova Scotia (c.1800), hurley developed into ice hockey.
Hornbeam	Tree *(Ostrya Virginiana)* native to Nova Scotia, with strong, durable hardwood, used to make wagon parts and Canada's first ice hockey sticks. Also called ironwood.
Horse Apples	Name given to frozen horse droppings, sometimes used by young hockeyists as pucks. Also called horse puckies.

Ice Carnival	Fancy-dress costume skating parties held in most skating rinks on an annual basis into the 1940s. Very competitive and popular.
Knickers	Over-the-knee trousers used in ice hockey until kneepads were devised, necessitating the use of short pants and long stockings.
Medallion	Large-size medal, used to signify championship, before trophies were introduced.
Mi'kmaq	Name of Nova Scotia's Natives.
Natural Ice	Water frozen by natural low temperature, as opposed to artificial ice, which is water frozen by chemical (artificial) means. Ice making by natural means limited the hockey season to less than three months a year.
Oochamkunutk	Name of Mi'kmaq field and ice game.
Point/Cover Point	Terms used in early days of ice hockey to describe the two positions now known as defence. They were placed one diagonally in front of the other.
Puck Hog	Before passing plays became scientific and popular, a good stickhandler capable of keeping the puck to himself for long periods of time was called a puck hog.
Puck Stop	A mountain-shaped piece of metal on the upper surfaces of goalkeeper's skate blades to prevent puck from passing between blade and boot. Invented by Starr Skate Company. Starr hockey skates could be ordered with or without puck stops.
Rink Rats	Boys who worked in covered rinks, scraping and shovelling snow from the ice, and who were "paid" with free ice time for skating and hockey or passes to games. They were replaced by the Zamboni machine, invented in California in 1949.
Rover	A flashy skater and high scoring hockeyist, usually the best on the team, who could play any position he wished. The position was devised in Nova Scotia and abandoned in 1913, reducing the number of players to six a side.
Shinny or Shinty	Scottish ice game resembling ice hockey, played with any number of players.
Singles	Metal blade skates (as opposed to tubes) which attached to boots with screws or rivets.
Skatist	One who skates; a skater.
Spring Skates	Metal skates with a special locking device that allowed them to be attached to soles and heels of boots with the flick of a lever.
Stickhandler	One who can shoot suddenly and accurately from either left or right, forehand or backhand.
Trophy	Fancy silver or gold cup or bowl used to signify supremacy in a sporting league. Introduced for ice hockey in 1890s to replace medallions.
Tube Skates	Blade skates imbedded in a lightweight tubular metal supporting structure, attached to boots with screws or rivets.
Wicket	Name of goalmouth; also called "flags," "goals," or "rickets," in early days of ice hockey.